Head, heart, hands
Life-transforming apologetics

"Steve West has done a magnificent job illustrating that Christianity is a life-transforming truth centred in Jesus. Steve skillfully sketches a plan for defending the Christian faith in a holistic manner.... Personally I have learned volumes from this book and am better equipped to declare and defend my faith. One can easily develop a greater appreciation of the wonder, beauty and uniqueness of the Christian worldview when it's seen in stark contrast to the various worldviews depicted in the book."

BOB PENHEAROW, *General editor and president*
Carey Outreach Ministries, Guelph, Ontario, Canada

"I am glad that Steve West has taken the opportunity to draw upon Andrew's own thoughts, ideas and writings in his development of this book on Christian apologetics.... he was one who had come fully to embrace and live the truths of which Steve writes."

STANLEY E. PORTER, *president, dean & professor*
McMaster Divinity College, Hamilton, Ontario, Canada

"As Andrew's wife, I was privileged to witness firsthand the life of a man who sought to make much of God. At the heart of his life was Christ, and the authority of his Word. As Andrew loved and studied apologetics, as well as Greek linguistics and biblical studies, it is fitting that Steve would choose to use Andrew's life as a practical example of being able to give a reason for the hope that is in us. I hope and pray this book will encourage every believer to know the gospel, be able to defend it and live it out as a testimony to God's amazing grace."

SUZANNE ROZALOWSKY
Canada

"I am not an apologetics person, but I do profit from reading good books on the subject. And Steve West's book, *Head, Heart, Hands* is one of the best I've read. It delivers a powerful argument for the Christian faith in easy to understand language. His chapter on the heart (emotions, morality and values) and then on the hands (loving service) are to me new and helpful arguments for the reality of the Christian faith."

JERRY BRIDGES, *author, speaker, staff member*
The Navigators, USA

"I really appreciate Steve's narrative use of the story of his friend Andrew. Weaving that story throughout the book is very helpful in making apologetics less dry, abstract and philosophical for the reader. I'm impressed with this book and am glad you are publishing it!"

PAUL E. ENGLE, *adjunct professor, North America,*
Carey International University of Theology,
former senior vice president, Zondervan, USA

HEAD, HEART, HANDS
Life-transforming apologetics

STEVEN D. WEST
GENERAL EDITOR: BOB PENHEAROW

CAREY
PRINTING PRESS

Published by
Carey Outreach Ministries Inc., Guelph, Ontario, Canada
www.careyoutreach.org

About us
Carey Printing Press is the publishing arm of Carey Outreach Ministries, an international Christian organization that provides theological training to spiritual leaders to shape the church and influence the nations.
General editor: Bob Penhearow

First published 2015
© 2015 Carey Printing Press. All rights reserved. This book may not be reproduced, in whole or in part, without written permission from the publishers.

Cover and book design: Janice Van Eck

All images: Shutterstock, public domain or the designer's archives.
Bible quotations: Unless otherwise indicated, all Scripture quotations are from The Holy Bible, New International Version,® NIV® Copyright © 1973, 1978, 1984, 2011 by Biblica, Inc.® Used by permission. All rights reserved worldwide.

Library and Archives Canada Cataloguing in Publication

West, Steven D., 1979–, author
    Head, heart, hands : life-transforming apologetics / Steven D. West.

ISBN 978-0-9876841-3-4 (paperback)

    1. Christianity—Philosophy. 2. Christianity—Psychology. 3. Christian life. I. Title.

BR100.W48 2015   230.01   C2015-905375-7

Andrew William Earl Rozalowsky

In memoriam
April 28, 1984–January 6, 2014

Jesus said to her, "I am the resurrection and the life. The one who believes in me will live, even though they die; and whoever lives by believing in me will never die. Do you believe this?" (John 11:25–26)

Contents

Foreword *by Stanley E. Porter*   xi
Preface *by Bob Penhearow*   xv
Acknowledgements   xix

    Introduction   1
1. What is the reason for our hope?   5
2. What is the Christian worldview?   21
3. How do I choose?   39
4. Is the resurrection of Jesus credible?   63
5. Christianity's great contradiction?   85
6. Christianity's great solution   107
    Interlude   127
7. Values, beauty and fulfillment   131
8. What does love do?   151

Epilogue   173
Appendix: A patient hope *by Andrew Rozalowsky*   177

Foreword

Andrew Rozalowsky was an exceptional young man. I don't know anyone who had the privilege of knowing Andrew well—whether that was a fellow student or professor or anyone else—who would say anything but that. I had the honour of being one of his seminary teachers during the last several years of Andrew's life, and I will always be thankful for the opportunity to have shared his life and academic adventure with him.

I still remember when Andrew first came to McMaster Divinity College as a potential student. Not only did he readily take on the challenge of a difficult Greek exegesis course as his first attempt at seminary education, but he excelled in it. Greek exegesis was definitely something that interested and got the intellectual juices flowing in Andrew. His love for the Bible was clear, and as I later found out, this love was evident from the time of his conversion as an adult until he died.

On the basis of his ability in that first exegesis course, we allowed Andrew to enroll in our rigorous M.A. program, where he also excelled.

Andrew was a pleasure to have in class. He was engaging, curious and always well prepared—having done his work and coming with plenty of questions for further discussion. Along the way, we began contemplating his plans for the future—the mission field, possible doctoral studies and other things. One of Andrew's great passions was the spread of the gospel to the Ukraine.

Once Andrew developed leukemia, there were many of us who did not know how this would affect Andrew and his desire for higher education. In some ways, his leukemia became further impetus for more intense study of the Bible and of theology. After he recovered from his first episode of leukemia, he returned to his studies, at first tentatively but with increasing fervour. He finished his course work and then started on his M.A. thesis. I was privileged to be his supervisor for this thesis work, a good chunk of which he had written by the time of his death.

I will never forget the day that I gave a plenary address at the inaugural meeting of the Evangelical Theological Society Ontario/Quebec region in September 2013. I don't remember the day so much for my paper but for my conversation with Andrew. My paper was the last of the day, and as I sat in the front row, awaiting my time to speak, I spoke with Andrew, who was sitting in the row behind, to encourage his teacher on the occasion. It was that day that Andrew admitted to himself that he was not feeling very well, and then decided to return to the doctor only to find out that he had a recurrence of the leukemia to which he would finally succumb.

Even in the hospital during his last illness, he was enthusiastically reading and studying. The table by his bed had a number of recent acquisitions on it. He knew that God was in control and that God had his plans for him—but Andrew wanted to be ready in the event that those plans included recovery from this bout of leukemia. Many of us followed Andrew throughout these last several years, as he blogged and wrote about what he was learning and what God was teaching him about his love, life, the Bible and so many more things.

I am glad that Steve West has taken the opportunity to draw upon Andrew's own thoughts, ideas and writings in his development of this book on Christian apologetics. Even though Andrew had majored in philosophy as an undergraduate, his Christianity was certainly not an abstract conception, but a fully embodied and completely relevant way of life. Andrew lived every day in obvious testimony to the living Christ who animated his very being.

One of the tangible ways that Andrew demonstrated his faith was his interest in making a reasonable presentation of the faith to others who had not had the good fortune to commit their lives to Christ—whoever that person may be, whether a fellow worker or a hospital attendant. This book captures some of those candid statements that give glimpses—unfortunately partial, though they are the best that we now have—of the Andrew Rozalowsky that we all remember so well. I encourage readers to consider the arguments that Steve makes in this book, with the help of Andrew and his own comments, and note that Andrew was one who had come fully to embrace and live the truths of which Steve writes.

Stanley E. Porter, Ph.D.
President and Dean
Professor of New Testament
Roy A. Hope Chair in Christian Worldview
McMaster Divinity College, Hamilton, Ontario

Preface

Salvation, the forgiveness of sins, is not in the hands of man, in eloquence of speech or in rational arguments alone. Salvation is ultimately in God's sovereign hands. The enabling power of the Holy Spirit at Pentecost transformed weak and frail vessels, such as the early disciples, into passionate, articulate, light-bearers. They boldly declared and defended their faith in the midst of darkness. They stood firm against vain philosophies, demolished the gods of the Greco-Roman world and stood confidently against principalities and powers in the cosmic realms. The apostle Paul, a transformed persecutor of the early church, declares, "I am not ashamed of the gospel, because it is the power of God that brings salvation" (Romans 1:16). The power of the gospel shakes kings and kingdoms, causes nations to rise and fall and transforms civilizations from generation to generation. The Holy Spirit alone is the life-giver and life-transformer—without him we can accomplish nothing. To God alone be the glory!

Yet, God's method is to use men and women, boys and girls, both in the past and in this present day. God has chosen to use broken, cracked, clay vessels such as ourselves, enabled by his Spirit, to defend and declare the wonders of his grace to a broken humanity. At best, we are instruments in God's hands. In this way, he delights to use our entire being to declare his glorious salvation. Our minds, hearts, hands and feet are all used by him to achieve his glory.

Dr. Steve West has done a magnificent job illustrating that Christianity is a life-transforming truth centred in Jesus. Steve skillfully sketches a plan for defending the Christian faith in a holistic manner. The first section of his work considers intellectual, rational and philosophical issues, which he deems the head (Chapters 2–6), then moves on to consider emotions, morality and values, which he refers to as the heart (Chapter 7). Steve then concludes with a combination of the mind and heart, which are to be engaged in loving service, which he rightly calls the hands (Chapter 8).

Steve cuts to the chase and unequivocally points out that Jesus alone is the central figure and only true key to life-transforming apologetics, that Jesus alone is the epicentre of our entire faith and hope, despite the trials and traumas that life can throw at us:

> In frailty and weakness we might go through times of despair and turmoil, but in the end our hope remains. The reason for our hope is not sunny skies, cancer-free bodies, ninety years of life or a good retirement plan. It is Jesus. Jesus, Jesus, Jesus. And when people ask the reason for our hope—no matter what the circumstances—Jesus is the one we must tell them about.

I especially delighted in the way Steve skillfully crafts the book to come alive in illustrating his cogent reasoning with a variety of earthy illustrations. From cover to cover, the story unravels the testimony of Andrew Rozalowsky, a close friend of Steve, whose life and eventual death boldly declared an unshakable faith in the resurrected Christ and a steadfast hope of glory.

Steve's closing statement is a wonderful summary of the entire book:

> Our hearts need to change so that our actions can change. We always act in accordance with our character: a godly character produces godly fruit, and an ungodly character produces ungodly

Head, heart, hands
Life-transforming apologetics

"Steve West has done a magnificent job illustrating that Christianity is a life-transforming truth centred in Jesus. Steve skillfully sketches a plan for defending the Christian faith in a holistic manner.... Personally I have learned volumes from this book and am better equipped to declare and defend my faith. One can easily develop a greater appreciation of the wonder, beauty and uniqueness of the Christian worldview when it's seen in stark contrast to the various worldviews depicted in the book."

BOB PENHEAROW, *General editor and president*
Carey Outreach Ministries, Guelph, Ontario, Canada

"I am glad that Steve West has taken the opportunity to draw upon Andrew's own thoughts, ideas and writings in his development of this book on Christian apologetics.... he was one who had come fully to embrace and live the truths of which Steve writes."

STANLEY E. PORTER, *president, dean & professor*
McMaster Divinity College, Hamilton, Ontario, Canada

"As Andrew's wife, I was privileged to witness firsthand the life of a man who sought to make much of God. At the heart of his life was Christ, and the authority of his Word. As Andrew loved and studied apologetics, as well as Greek linguistics and biblical studies, it is fitting that Steve would choose to use Andrew's life as a practical example of being able to give a reason for the hope that is in us. I hope and pray this book will encourage every believer to know the gospel, be able to defend it and live it out as a testimony to God's amazing grace."

SUZANNE ROZALOWSKY
Canada

"I am not an apologetics person, but I do profit from reading good books on the subject. And Steve West's book, *Head, Heart, Hands* is one of the best I've read. It delivers a powerful argument for the Christian faith in easy to understand language. His chapter on the heart (emotions, morality and values) and then on the hands (loving service) are to me new and helpful arguments for the reality of the Christian faith."

JERRY BRIDGES, *author, speaker, staff member*
The Navigators, USA

"I really appreciate Steve's narrative use of the story of his friend Andrew. Weaving that story throughout the book is very helpful in making apologetics less dry, abstract and philosophical for the reader. I'm impressed with this book and am glad you are publishing it!"

PAUL E. ENGLE, *adjunct professor, North America,*
Carey International University of Theology,
former senior vice president, Zondervan, USA

HEAD, HEART, HANDS
Life-transforming apologetics

STEVEN D. WEST
GENERAL EDITOR: BOB PENHEAROW

CAREY
PRINTING PRESS

Published by
Carey Outreach Ministries Inc., Guelph, Ontario, Canada
www.careyoutreach.org

About us
Carey Printing Press is the publishing arm of Carey Outreach Ministries, an international Christian organization that provides theological training to spiritual leaders to shape the church and influence the nations.
General editor: Bob Penhearow

First published 2015
© 2015 Carey Printing Press. All rights reserved. This book may not be reproduced, in whole or in part, without written permission from the publishers.

Cover and book design: Janice Van Eck

All images: Shutterstock, public domain or the designer's archives.
Bible quotations: Unless otherwise indicated, all Scripture quotations are from The Holy Bible, New International Version,® NIV® Copyright © 1973, 1978, 1984, 2011 by Biblica, Inc.® Used by permission. All rights reserved worldwide.

Library and Archives Canada Cataloguing in Publication

West, Steven D., 1979–, author
    Head, heart, hands : life-transforming apologetics / Steven D. West.

ISBN 978-0-9876841-3-4 (paperback)

    1. Christianity—Philosophy. 2. Christianity—Psychology. 3. Christian life. I. Title.

BR100.W48 2015   230.01   C2015-905375-7

Andrew William Earl Rozalowsky

In memoriam
April 28, 1984–January 6, 2014

Jesus said to her, "I am the resurrection and the life. The one who believes in me will live, even though they die; and whoever lives by believing in me will never die. Do you believe this?" (John 11:25–26)

Contents

Foreword *by Stanley E. Porter*		xi
Preface *by Bob Penhearow*		xv
Acknowledgements		xix
	Introduction	1
1	What is the reason for our hope?	5
2	What is the Christian worldview?	21
3	How do I choose?	39
4	Is the resurrection of Jesus credible?	63
5	Christianity's great contradiction?	85
6	Christianity's great solution	107
	Interlude	127
7	Values, beauty and fulfillment	131
8	What does love do?	151
	Epilogue	173
	Appendix: A patient hope *by Andrew Rozalowsky*	177

Foreword

Andrew Rozalowsky was an exceptional young man. I don't know anyone who had the privilege of knowing Andrew well—whether that was a fellow student or professor or anyone else—who would say anything but that. I had the honour of being one of his seminary teachers during the last several years of Andrew's life, and I will always be thankful for the opportunity to have shared his life and academic adventure with him.

I still remember when Andrew first came to McMaster Divinity College as a potential student. Not only did he readily take on the challenge of a difficult Greek exegesis course as his first attempt at seminary education, but he excelled in it. Greek exegesis was definitely something that interested and got the intellectual juices flowing in Andrew. His love for the Bible was clear, and as I later found out, this love was evident from the time of his conversion as an adult until he died.

On the basis of his ability in that first exegesis course, we allowed Andrew to enroll in our rigorous M.A. program, where he also excelled.

Andrew was a pleasure to have in class. He was engaging, curious and always well prepared—having done his work and coming with plenty of questions for further discussion. Along the way, we began contemplating his plans for the future—the mission field, possible doctoral studies and other things. One of Andrew's great passions was the spread of the gospel to the Ukraine.

Once Andrew developed leukemia, there were many of us who did not know how this would affect Andrew and his desire for higher education. In some ways, his leukemia became further impetus for more intense study of the Bible and of theology. After he recovered from his first episode of leukemia, he returned to his studies, at first tentatively but with increasing fervour. He finished his course work and then started on his M.A. thesis. I was privileged to be his supervisor for this thesis work, a good chunk of which he had written by the time of his death.

I will never forget the day that I gave a plenary address at the inaugural meeting of the Evangelical Theological Society Ontario/Quebec region in September 2013. I don't remember the day so much for my paper but for my conversation with Andrew. My paper was the last of the day, and as I sat in the front row, awaiting my time to speak, I spoke with Andrew, who was sitting in the row behind, to encourage his teacher on the occasion. It was that day that Andrew admitted to himself that he was not feeling very well, and then decided to return to the doctor only to find out that he had a recurrence of the leukemia to which he would finally succumb.

Even in the hospital during his last illness, he was enthusiastically reading and studying. The table by his bed had a number of recent acquisitions on it. He knew that God was in control and that God had his plans for him—but Andrew wanted to be ready in the event that those plans included recovery from this bout of leukemia. Many of us followed Andrew throughout these last several years, as he blogged and wrote about what he was learning and what God was teaching him about his love, life, the Bible and so many more things.

I am glad that Steve West has taken the opportunity to draw upon Andrew's own thoughts, ideas and writings in his development of this book on Christian apologetics. Even though Andrew had majored in philosophy as an undergraduate, his Christianity was certainly not an abstract conception, but a fully embodied and completely relevant way of life. Andrew lived every day in obvious testimony to the living Christ who animated his very being.

One of the tangible ways that Andrew demonstrated his faith was his interest in making a reasonable presentation of the faith to others who had not had the good fortune to commit their lives to Christ—whoever that person may be, whether a fellow worker or a hospital attendant. This book captures some of those candid statements that give glimpses—unfortunately partial, though they are the best that we now have—of the Andrew Rozalowsky that we all remember so well. I encourage readers to consider the arguments that Steve makes in this book, with the help of Andrew and his own comments, and note that Andrew was one who had come fully to embrace and live the truths of which Steve writes.

Stanley E. Porter, Ph.D.
President and Dean
Professor of New Testament
Roy A. Hope Chair in Christian Worldview
McMaster Divinity College, Hamilton, Ontario

Preface

Salvation, the forgiveness of sins, is not in the hands of man, in eloquence of speech or in rational arguments alone. Salvation is ultimately in God's sovereign hands. The enabling power of the Holy Spirit at Pentecost transformed weak and frail vessels, such as the early disciples, into passionate, articulate, light-bearers. They boldly declared and defended their faith in the midst of darkness. They stood firm against vain philosophies, demolished the gods of the Greco-Roman world and stood confidently against principalities and powers in the cosmic realms. The apostle Paul, a transformed persecutor of the early church, declares, "I am not ashamed of the gospel, because it is the power of God that brings salvation" (Romans 1:16). The power of the gospel shakes kings and kingdoms, causes nations to rise and fall and transforms civilizations from generation to generation. The Holy Spirit alone is the life-giver and life-transformer—without him we can accomplish nothing. To God alone be the glory!

Yet, God's method is to use men and women, boys and girls, both in the past and in this present day. God has chosen to use broken, cracked, clay vessels such as ourselves, enabled by his Spirit, to defend and declare the wonders of his grace to a broken humanity. At best, we are instruments in God's hands. In this way, he delights to use our entire being to declare his glorious salvation. Our minds, hearts, hands and feet are all used by him to achieve his glory.

Dr. Steve West has done a magnificent job illustrating that Christianity is a life-transforming truth centred in Jesus. Steve skillfully sketches a plan for defending the Christian faith in a holistic manner. The first section of his work considers intellectual, rational and philosophical issues, which he deems the head (Chapters 2–6), then moves on to consider emotions, morality and values, which he refers to as the heart (Chapter 7). Steve then concludes with a combination of the mind and heart, which are to be engaged in loving service, which he rightly calls the hands (Chapter 8).

Steve cuts to the chase and unequivocally points out that Jesus alone is the central figure and only true key to life-transforming apologetics, that Jesus alone is the epicentre of our entire faith and hope, despite the trials and traumas that life can throw at us:

> In frailty and weakness we might go through times of despair and turmoil, but in the end our hope remains. The reason for our hope is not sunny skies, cancer-free bodies, ninety years of life or a good retirement plan. It is Jesus. Jesus, Jesus, Jesus. And when people ask the reason for our hope—no matter what the circumstances—Jesus is the one we must tell them about.

I especially delighted in the way Steve skillfully crafts the book to come alive in illustrating his cogent reasoning with a variety of earthy illustrations. From cover to cover, the story unravels the testimony of Andrew Rozalowsky, a close friend of Steve, whose life and eventual death boldly declared an unshakable faith in the resurrected Christ and a steadfast hope of glory.

Steve's closing statement is a wonderful summary of the entire book:

> Our hearts need to change so that our actions can change. We always act in accordance with our character: a godly character produces godly fruit, and an ungodly character produces ungodly

fruit. Gospel change occurs internally, but it can't help but be manifested externally. God transforms our hearts, and in so doing he transforms our hands. Since people can't see inside of us, the strength of our witness and defence of the faith will hinge on how we live. Perhaps it is time for all apologists to see how Paul's statement that, "The only thing that counts is faith expressing itself in love" (Galatians 5:6b) applies to the practice of apologetics.

Personally I have learned volumes from this book and am better equipped to declare and defend my faith. One can easily develop a greater appreciation of the wonder, beauty and uniqueness of the Christian worldview when it's seen in stark contrast to the various worldviews depicted in the book.

My prayer is that our gracious, sovereign God uses my head, heart, hands and feet to declare and defend his life-transforming, glorious truth. *Soli Deo gloria!*

Bob Penhearow, D.Min.
General editor and president
Carey Outreach Ministries

Acknowledgements

This book was written in community, and I am indebted to more people than I can name. On a broad level, I would like to thank the faculties and students at both Heritage Seminary (Cambridge, Ontario) and Toronto Baptist Seminary—I have learned a great deal from all of you. I am also thankful to Crestwicke Baptist Church in Guelph for enabling me to teach and minister in fields outside of our local congregation. This has meant a great deal of extra work for my colleague Sam McCallum, and I appreciate the magnificent job he does as a true shepherd of God's people. My wife Heather and daughters Charlotte and Brooklyn patiently put up with my schedule and periods of preoccupation without complaint. I am incredibly blessed to have these three lovely and loving girls at the core of my life.

More specific thanks is due to those who read drafts of this book at various stages and provided comments and encouragement (as well as some fairly strong criticisms!). Your willingness to help was a great motivator. I am most grateful to Linda Lumsden, John Bell, Sarah

Primmer, Drs. Shayne and Margaret Love (particularly for their help with statistics and mathematical equations) and Shona Blatch. A special thanks is owed to Jesskah Farquharson for transcribing Andrew's sermon and for editing and cleaning up my original draft. This book has been greatly improved by her careful work.

Graham Watt has been a tireless supporter and source of encouragement, as well as very patient during the process of coordinating print publication with electronic release for Power to Change. It is a special privilege to have this work going out to the universities. Stan Porter has taken an enormous amount of time to give me advice and help in regards to publishing this book. I know how much Andrew esteemed his time with Dr. Porter, and I am personally grateful for the time and kindness that Stan has given to me.

Dr. Bob Penhearow has received this book with great enthusiasm, and I am very thankful for his encouragement and support. Bob added the "Remember, Reflect, Rejoice" sections at the end of each chapter. Through Carey Ministries, this book is scheduled to be printed and distributed to pastors and church leaders in different countries around the world. (They will receive the book for free.) Janice Van Eck has done a wonderful job for Carey Ministries in preparing this book for publication.

This book would not have been possible without the incredible life and legacy of Andrew Rozalowsky. His permission and encouragement to write this book kept me going. Although he was never able to read it, I trust it would meet with his approval. I have no doubt that he would have had some very helpful criticisms to make it better. I am also aware that the best parts of this book are the sections where I quote from his writings.

Without the permission and encouragement of Suzanne Rozalowsky, I would never have published this book. Suzanne's endorsement has been very special, and I can only hope that this work represents Andrew in a fitting way. I also hope that Jacob and Daniel will appreciate this book when they are older. Thank you, Suzanne. You and your boys are a blessing and a testimony to the glory and grace of God.

Introduction

Many Christians worry that they do not know how to effectively communicate the truth of the gospel. More to the point, many Christians fear that they are not equipped to answer skeptical objections to their faith. They know the truth, but they don't know how to defend it. Although Christianity is philosophically defensible, it is a mistake to think that the only way it can be defended is intellectually. Christian truth needs to be defended rationally, logically and philosophically, as well as emotionally, experientially and ethically. The truth of Jesus is defended by thoughts, feelings, words and deeds. God has designed us to defend his truth with our head, heart and hands enabled and empowered by his Spirit.

This book is based on the premise that Christianity is a *life-transforming* truth. It is life-transforming because knowing God through Jesus Christ completely changes someone's life. In fact, it is only when someone comes to know God through Jesus Christ that they really begin to live in the first place. Christianity is *truth* because it corresponds to the way things actually are—it accurately represents reality, and as a result, it is trustworthy, reliable and worthy of acceptance. Most importantly, Christianity is a life-transforming truth because it is founded on Jesus Christ, who is *the* life-transforming truth. He is the truth that sets us free.[1]

Christianity is not merely an intellectually coherent system of beliefs—it is more than that, not less. The content of the Christian faith can be expressed in consistent axioms and propositions, but at its centre is the person of Jesus: it is true because he is the Truth. Jesus always *speaks* the truth, but he also *does* the truth, because he *is* the truth. All of his actions display the right and the good: in other words, Jesus' life shows us the truth about how we are to live. His actions reveal the nature of reality as truly as his words illumine it. Jesus is the consummate teacher: he teaches the truth by his every word and in his every deed. Truth is seen as well as heard.

This principle applies to Jesus' followers. Christians proclaim and defend—or undercut and damage—the credibility of their testimony by both their words and their actions. Defending the faith requires cogent thinking and a clearly articulated case. Furthermore, when the integrity of the Christian faith is on trial, vital testimony is supplied by character witnesses. More precisely, it is the Christian's *character* that *witnesses*. If someone claims to have discovered a life-transforming truth, but their life bears no signs of transformation—or even the initial beginnings of a process of transformation—then their case is rightly met with skepticism. A changed life, however, indicates a life-changing discovery has truly been made.

In our contemporary society, there are not too many people making the extraordinary mistake of believing that Christianity is merely a set of religious propositions. There are, however, a number who are under the equally erroneous impression that Christianity is only concerned with the soul, and completely ignores the mind. Christianity is nothing if not holistic: it affects the heart and the soul, and in so doing it affects what we do in the body. One of the truly wonderful things about Christianity is that it makes people whole. Our society is becoming more and more aware of the importance of holistic medicine: a totally holistic cure is only available from the Great Physician.

---

[1] John 8:32.

Christianity is the place where the universal and the particular merge. The truth of Christianity is universal: *it is true in every time and every place*. The claim *Jesus is Lord* is not merely true locally, or only in some countries, or even only for some people. *Jesus is Lord* is a universal truth. It is not a matter of perspective. Neither is it based on pragmatics —whether or not you think that believing that Jesus is Lord is beneficial is entirely beside the point. He is Lord whether you like it or not, whether you think that's a good thing or not, whether you love him or hate him; *Jesus is Lord* represents an objective fact that is universally true. All the major doctrines of Christianity are universal claims.

Our lives, however, are particular. We are local and individual. Christianity integrates universal truth into particular people: it brings together the objective and the subjective. The universal, objective truth of God is planted deep inside particular subjects—and it doesn't lie dormant. The seed of God's universal truth germinates, grows, buds, flowers and produces fruit—particular fruit on a particular tree. Defending the truth of Christianity requires digging down to examine its truth-foundations, i.e. its universal root, but the fruit should be evidence that is plainly visible. The absence of fruit often indicates a defective root system. Christians, therefore, should learn to intellectually defend the universal truths of God, as well as cultivate the fruit of spiritual and moral goodness. The Christian faith is *truth* and *life-transforming*.

One implication of this reality is that Christianity can—and should—be defended by both analyzing its universal root and inspecting its fruit. However, the fruit is particular, not universal. So Christianity should be defended intellectually as something that all people should accept (because it's true), but it should also be defended by pointing to *particular examples*. We all do this intuitively: an atheist points out particular examples of hypocrisy or immorality in the church, and Christians point out particular examples of heroic self-sacrifice and virtue. We will look at hypocrisy in a later chapter; for now the point is that we oscillate between discussing universal principles and noting particular examples. My contention is that the faith needs to be defended in regards to both universals and particulars—and some particulars really help us see the reality of the universals.

As a result of this belief, in this book I am going to sketch a plan for defending the Christian faith in a *holistic* manner. In this defence, we will consider intellectual, rational and philosophical issues (*the head*, Chapters 2–6), as well as emotions, morality and values (*the heart*, Chapter 7) and then take a quick look at how the mind and heart should motivate us to perform practical acts of loving service (*the hands*, Chapter 8).

I am also going to weave the particular example of one individual into the fabric of the argument. His name is Andrew Rozalowsky. When I began to write this book, no one on earth knew if he was going to live for more than a few weeks. The day I finished a draft introduction to this book, Andrew died.

What is the reason for our hope?

My friend Andrew Rozalowsky is twenty-nine years old, five years younger than I am. His oldest son is three-and-a-half, about five years younger than my oldest daughter. His youngest son is not quite one year old, about five years younger than my youngest daughter. His wife is similarly younger than my wife. As I write this sentence, Andrew is lying sedated on a hospital bed, hooked up to a ventilator, fighting a serious infection that is threatening to end his life. The infection would not be life-threatening if his immune system was not so compromised by the strong regime of chemotherapy he has needed over the last few months. Andrew has an aggressive form of blood cancer: leukemia. Approximately two years ago he received the diagnosis, but his first round of treatment successfully put the cancer into remission. At present, he has finished his second round of treatment, this time with the most intense medication available. Yet, despite all our medical technology and the best efforts of an excellent medical staff, the cancer has not been destroyed.

Andrew's only medical chance is to be enrolled in a clinical trial. When I discussed the possibilities with him, he was lucidly aware that *clinical trial* is a sanitized way of saying *experiment*: it is his last chance for life. There are multiple reasons not to be optimistic. First, he needs to qualify as a fitting candidate who is compatible with the stem cell treatment the trial is conducting. Second, he needs to reach a certain threshold of physical strength to be able to receive the treatment. Third, the very nature of the trial is such that the prognosis—even if the procedure goes well—is uncertain at best: it seems highly unlikely statistically that Andrew will qualify for the treatment and that it will produce a successful outcome.

Despite all of this, the one thing that characterizes Andrew's life is a deep, confident, unconquerable hope. It is not the hope of a supposedly indomitable human spirit or the hope of a godlike medical system finding the cure for his cancer before it's too late. It is not a fool's hope that ignores circumstances and pretends that "it just can't happen to me." Andrew's hope is sure and certain because it is not grounded in himself or human expertise. His hope is in God through Jesus Christ. This is why whenever he's asked how he's doing—regardless of how nauseous he is from the chemo, how weak he feels or how much emotional turmoil he is in thinking about his family—he replies that he is fine, because *his hope is in Jesus*.

Lest this be misunderstood, it needs to be said that Andrew rejects all health, wealth and prosperity preaching. He does not believe that God is definitely going to heal him (although he believes that God *can* do so if he chooses). Actually, Andrew *does* believe that God is going to completely heal him, but he knows that such ultimate healing awaits the new heavens and the new earth. Andrew does not know if he will live or die in the next few days or in the next few decades, but his assurance lies in knowing that when he dies he will die safely in the arms of his Lord and Saviour Jesus Christ.

As people have observed this attitude in him during this difficult and painful time, they often ask how he does it. They want to know the reason for the hope he has. So when he's asked, Andrew tells people he's fine because he knows Jesus. God is in control of all that is taking place: Jesus has never let him down, and never will. He has hope in eternal life because of what the Lord Jesus Christ has done for him in paying for his sins on the cross and conquering death through his triumphant resurrection from the grave. When he dies (whether before turning thirty or during old age in a nursing home) his spirit will immediately be ushered into the presence of the Lord. His faith will be sight. In spite of a cancer that may prove stronger than his body, Andrew has confidence in the sovereign Lord of heaven and earth.

When Andrew talks about the hope he has because of Jesus, people listen. His amazing attitude of trust and hope—rather than bitterness, anger or despair—serves to make the depth of his hope clear. People might disagree that his hope is well-founded, but they cannot deny that his hope is pervasive and runs deep into the inner recesses of his being. As a result, both his life and his verbal testimony work together as a powerful witness to the gospel of Jesus Christ.

Besides our relatively similar ages and family situations, Andrew and I also have a mutual interest in the academic study of Christianity. He has the makings of a fine scholar, specializing in the study of the New Testament (particularly focused on Greek linguistics). He also has a side interest in apologetics, the subject that deals with defending the validity of the Christian faith. Apologetics is the subject in which I've done my academic work. Before Andrew's leukemia reasserted itself, we had been talking about doing some shared work on the relationship between the New Testament and the discipline of apologetics. Although I don't know if we'll ever be able to work on that project together, I do know that I would not be writing this particular book if it were not for him.

As I've seen how Andrew has handled himself over the last few months, and as I've heard him speak so clearly about his hope in Jesus, it has struck me how much his attitude serves as an excellent apologetic for the faith. His hope in the face of probable death speaks volumes. What has really impacted me is how much the defence of the faith is not merely a matter of reciting rational arguments for our faith. There is definitely a place for providing intellectual reasons for our hope, but a fully-orbed defence of our faith requires more than that. An effective apologetic will combine intellectual, emotional and practical elements into a cohesive whole.

NARRATIVE APOLOGETICS

Andrew was hopeful not only up until the very end, but *through* the very end. The bulletin from his funeral has adorned my desk for almost half a year now. On the front there is a picture of Andrew, a cross, and the words: "In Loving Memory of Andrew William Earl Rozalowsky. Faithful Servant of Jesus Christ. April 28, 1984, to January 6, 2014." If Christianity is a universal truth that makes claims about ultimate reality, eternity and things of infinite importance, it should be enough for life and more than enough for death. God's Word is the universal; Andrew will be the particular example.

When I told Andrew that I was thinking about writing this book, I said that I wanted to explore the relationship between the intellectual, emotional and practical elements that are required for an effective defence of the faith. I asked permission to use some of his social media posts and other writings as illustrations and examples of the principles under discussion. He emailed me from his hospital bed and said, "Permission granted. *Soli Deo Gloria* [To God alone be the glory]." To follow his desire for God alone to receive the glory, I am going to refer to his life and writings only when they underscore a particular point or help clarify a broad apologetic principle. The result is that the reader need not know Andrew personally in order to benefit from the discussion in this book.

This book is not intended to be an encyclopedia of answers to every possible skeptical objection. It is a pointer, a sketch. If I had to give a title to the method, I would like to coin the phrase *narrative apologetics*. In other words, this is an exercise in comparing stories (i.e. narratives). The question is, *Which story is intelligible? Which narrative is coherent? Which way of looking at the world is holistically satisfying?* I am not pretending to compare every narrative or worldview in the following pages. If successful, this work will provide a few tools and a few hints for constructing a sound defence of the faith. Not every step in every argument is spelled out, but I believe that the general conclusions can be rigorously philosophically defended.

In his own words, this is how Andrew Rozalowsky expressed his personal hope—the hope that all Christians share:

On December 9th, 2004, I trusted Christ. Here is my brief reflection nine years later:

Nine years ago tonight I:
repented of my sins/

knelt at his feet/
wept for joy/
trusted Jesus/
believed on the gospel/
was called by God/
was forgiven by God/
was transferred into his Kingdom/
was made free/
was adopted as a child of God/
was justified/
was redeemed/
began to follow Jesus/
died to self/
was given hope/
was made alive in Christ/
was renewed in heart/
was given the Spirit/
sin became disgusting/
Christ became glorious//

Nine years later in the face of possible death:
Christ remains glorious/
Christ remains my joy/
Christ remains my hope/

(To the theologians in the crowd, I have not tried to purposely organize the list into any ordo salutis*).*

Right up until the time he passed away, when people asked Andrew how he was doing, he would tell them that he was fine because his hope was in Jesus. Imagine a skeptical person asking him how he could keep being filled with hope as time dragged on and medical wisdom failed and the cancer took a larger and larger toll on his body. In cold, clinical, statistical analysis, there wasn't much hope that the cancer would be vanquished. As previously mentioned, Andrew was not a believer in health, wealth and prosperity preaching. He didn't have an unbiblical hope that no matter how bad things got, God would swoop down at the last moment and miraculously restore him to health and strength. No, Andrew's hope was not based on avoiding death for a few more years. His hope was in Jesus Christ. His hope was in the *person who gives eternal life*. So when people asked him why he had quiet confidence and could face whatever the future would hold—whether life or death—he told them that the reason for the hope that he had was nothing more nor less than the Lord Jesus Christ.

CHRISTIAN HOPE

Christian apologists love to quote 1 Peter 3:15–16:

> But in your hearts revere Christ as Lord. Always be prepared to give an answer to everyone who asks you to give the reason for the hope that you have. But do this with gentleness and respect, keeping a clear conscience, so that those who speak maliciously against your good behavior in Christ may be ashamed of their slander.

> ***apologia***
> *(Greek) n.*
> a reasoned defence.

This passage speaks of giving an answer (the Greek word is *apologia*, which denotes a reasoned defence) to anyone who asks the believer to explain why they are full of hope. Apologists often seem to take Peter's words as a command to study academic apologetics. This is not, however, what Peter meant.

For every believer

For starters, 1 Peter is written for *every* believer. Every Christian, at some level, is expected to be able to do what these verses instruct. But many of the people who first heard this letter read aloud in their church were illiterate. One can only imagine the percentage of Christians throughout the history of the church who have been poorly educated or illiterate. Apologists need to remember that the average Christian does not have a graduate degree, and around the world many believers—like nonbelievers—have little or no education at all. One week ago, I was visiting with my grandmother, and she mentioned in passing that she had never been in a high school until she went to one of my mom's high school events. I say this respectfully, but if 1 Peter 3:15–16 meant that my grandmother had to have an answer ready for every question an atheist with a Ph.D. in philosophy could ask her, she would definitely not be fulfilling the requirements of the passage. Clearly, Peter's focus lies in a different direction.

The longer someone studies apologetics, the easier it is for them to get confused as to what the reason for their hope actually is. The reason we have hope is because of God himself—it is not because of our arguments that defend his existence. We have hope because of the resurrection of Jesus Christ from the dead—the reason for our hope is not our arguments for the historicity of the resurrection. What Peter is saying is this: we should be prepared to tell anyone at any time that Jesus Christ is the reason for the hope that we have. And that, thankfully, is something even an illiterate Christian can do.

Now of course conversations can grow in complexity. I am not suggesting that there is no place for defending the faith at the most rigorous academic levels. I am thankful for the brilliant Christian academics who are capable of showing the cogency and rationality of the faith in spite of all the challenges brought against it. I even believe that one way of applying 1 Peter 3:15–16 in our contemporary context is by encouraging some people to become professional apologists. But such Christian thinkers are exceptional, and such specialized study and knowledge is not necessary for the vast majority of believers. What Peter is saying is much simpler. When people ask the reason for your hope, you are to point them to Jesus Christ. Tell them how what he has done for you gives you hope. When you do, make sure it is with gentleness and respect, so that your attitude matches your message.

The wider context of suffering

Too often, 1 Peter 3:15–16 is quoted outside of its context. At a minimum, sentences need to be read in their paragraphs. Since paragraphs build on one another, the meaning of a sentence is partially dependent on the larger unit in which it's found. These larger units need to be interpreted in the context of the whole book where they are located. Practically, this means that understanding 1 Peter 3:15–16 requires reading it in the context of Peter's letter as a whole. When we take the time to read the whole letter, a very clear picture emerges that allows us to properly interpret what it means to give the reason for the hope that is in us, and why we might be asked for that reason in the first place.

One of the clear themes in 1 Peter is that the recipients of this letter are suffering. They are being unjustly discriminated against and even overtly persecuted. It is essential to recognize that they are suffering *because of their faith*. Everyone experiences pain and loss, but these believers are going through painful trials as a direct result of identifying themselves with Christ. They are at risk of losing economic security, friendships, respect, freedom and possibly even their lives, if they continue to maintain their commitment to the gospel of Jesus. Yet, in spite of suffering for the name of Jesus, Peter knows that God's children can persevere and rejoice in great hope. At this stage in his life Peter has personally suffered a large amount of persecution (partially recorded in the Book of Acts), yet he has continued to preach with joy and boldness in the name of Jesus. Believers are not to expect that they will be exempted from trials: they are expected—and empowered—to rejoice through them.

The Roman emperor, Nero (reign A.D. 54-68), was known for his virulent persecution of the early Christians, many of whom were converted through the apostles' preaching recorded in the book of Acts.

In several places Peter makes it clear that some of his audience are suffering already, and many others will begin to suffer in the near future. Some believers will be falsely and slanderously accused of wrong doing (1 Peter 2:12; 2:15; 3:16). In other cases, believers will be persecuted because they refuse to join in with those who are doing wrong (1 Peter 2:20; 3:13-14; 4:4,12-19). In these cases, the followers of Jesus are simply being treated like their Master before them. Peter not only reminds his readers that Jesus suffered for being righteous, but he did so in a way that demonstrated complete trust that God would set things right in due time (1 Peter 2:21-25; 4:1). Peter reminds his readers that in persecution, as in all else, the attitude of Jesus is something to be imitated.

We are not, however, called to just grin and bear it, no matter what "it" is. Nor are we called to suffer just to show that we can suffer with dignified, quiet strength. Christian joy in suffering for Jesus' sake is linked to his glory, the strengthening of our faith and our final eternal reward. Peter tells us that our faith is far more valuable than gold, and trials are a means that God uses to refine and purify our faith (1 Peter 1:7). As our faith becomes stronger and purer, we become more useful here in this world, and also more prepared for the world to come.

One of the reasons we can rejoice in suffering for the gospel today is that our faith sees our future eschatological glory: we are going to see Jesus, and on that day we will be rewarded. Not only is this the case, but from an eternal perspective our suffering is only for a very short period of time. In Peter's words, "And the God of all grace, who called you to his eternal glory in Christ, after you have suffered a little while, will himself restore you and make you strong, firm and steadfast" (1 Peter 5:10). Even now, God gives us supernatural strength, but after just a little time, a quick blink of the eye, we are brought into the consummation of eternal glory in Christ.

Now that we have briefly sketched out this theme in 1 Peter, we can understand more accurately the immediate context of 3:15–16. Instead of cutting the "apologetic" theme verses from the paragraph where they're found, we'll read the whole paragraph (verses 13–17):

> Who is going to harm you if you are eager to do good? But even if you should suffer for what is right, you are blessed. "Do not fear their threats; do not be frightened." But in your hearts revere Christ as Lord. Always be prepared to give an answer to everyone who asks you to give the reason for the hope that you have. But do this with gentleness and respect, keeping a clear conscience, so that those who speak maliciously against your good behavior in Christ may be ashamed of their slander. For it is better, if it is God's will, to suffer for doing good than for doing evil.

First Peter 3:15 is located in a paragraph that is dealing with Peter's wider theme of suffering for the sake of Jesus and righteousness. He tells his audience not to worry or be fearful if they are being persecuted for doing what's right. Far better to suffer for doing right than to suffer for doing wrong! Far better to suffer the wrath of mortals than the wrath of the Immortal. Those who are consciously honouring Jesus as the Lord of their lives will strive to be obedient to him, regardless of the consequences in this world. With gentleness and respect, persecutors—and all others who view our hope-filled suffering—will be answered. When winsome verbal testimony is combined with a gentle attitude and virtuous living, the result will be a powerful witness to the world.

It is difficult to know if Peter is describing the believer's interrogator as ridiculing them or making a serious inquiry. Perhaps it is a sarcastic challenge: "Your religion and stubbornness just cost you your livelihood! Why won't you just sacrifice to the trade guild's goddess? What makes you and your god better than anyone else? Seriously, why won't you just give your yearly offering to the idol? How great can your god be when he can't even help you keep your job? Why are you still clinging to this ridiculous hope of yours?"

Or, more positively, perhaps the inquirer is seriously intrigued. Perhaps the Christian response to suffering for Jesus is something they find compelling, or baffling or challenging. Maybe their questioning would be softer and more earnest: "I don't know how you're holding up like this. I could never go through what you're experiencing without breaking under the stress. Where does your strength come from? How can you be okay, given all that people have done to you? Why are you so confident in your God?" Either way, the believer who is suffering for righteousness is expected to give an answer.

A living hope
We do not need to guess what Peter expects his readers to say. Peter had already written in this letter about the true reason for our hope. After the letter's introduction, he plunges right in:

> Praise be to the God and Father of our Lord Jesus Christ! In his great mercy he has given us new birth into a living hope through the resurrection of Jesus Christ from the dead, and into an inheritance that can never perish, spoil or fade. This inheritance is kept in heaven for you, who through faith are shielded by God's power until the coming of the salvation that is ready to be revealed in the last time. In all this you greatly rejoice, though now for a little while you may have had to suffer grief in all kinds of trials" (1 Peter 1:3–6).

In this paragraph alone we have more than enough reason to maintain our hope throughout our entire lives, no matter what we face. Peter even goes so far as to say that, in God's mercy, we have been born into a *living* hope. Our new lives in Christ are characterized by a pulsating, exciting, growing hope: it is a hope that is alive. Persecution cannot kill it. It does not die with our bodies. It does not ebb away when we breathe our last. It cannot be beaten out of us, nor driven away by insults, nor put to flight by the worst of circumstances.

This living hope is ours because of God's merciful plan of salvation. Death cannot destroy our hope because our hope is rooted in the resurrection of Jesus Christ. Our hope is that, by his resurrection, Jesus killed death. Since our hope is based on the death of death, death cannot be the death of our hope! Christian hope is in the One who conquered death. Even though we die physically, our spirits go to be with the Lord, and one day in the future we will be resurrected in glorified, physical bodies. For the believer, death is never the last word—Jesus is. And where Jesus is, there we have an everlasting reward. Even now, we are shielded by God's power (i.e. we are going to make it to glory come what may), but one day we will go into his holy presence and experience the fullness of our salvation. This eternal perspective, this grace, this hope, this Lord—this is why we can rejoice when we suffer for his name.

All of these blessings are grounded in what God has done for us in his Son, the Lord Jesus Christ. Rather obviously, Jesus could not have been resurrected from the dead if he did not die. Jesus' death on the cross and his resurrection are both absolutely necessary for salvation. As Peter writes,

> For you know that it was not with perishable things such as silver or gold that you were redeemed from the empty way of life handed down to you from your ancestors, but with the precious blood of Christ, a lamb without blemish or defect. He was chosen before the creation of the world, but was revealed in these last times for your sake. Through him you believe in God, who raised him from the dead and glorified him, and so your faith and hope are in God (1 Peter 1:18–21).

When Jesus died on the cross he died as a real man who had never sinned in thought, word, motive or deed. Not only did he never do anything wrong, he also fulfilled all of his moral, spiritual and societal obligations. God the Father was perfectly pleased in all that Jesus was and all that Jesus did. At the end of his life, Jesus willingly chose to die, not for his own sins (since he had none), but for the sins of others. The reason he came to earth in the first place was to live and die for the sake of lost and hopeless sinners.

In the Old Testament, the Israelites would offer prescribed sacrifices to God. Some of the sacrifices very clearly illustrated that death was the right punishment for sin. The great problem was that everyone was a sinner, and thus, logically, everyone stood justly condemned to die. Reprieve could only come through a substitute: the only way a sinner could escape death was for someone to die in their place.

Over the centuries animals were sacrificed as substitutes, but animal blood could never take away human sin. The death of a bull or goat or lamb could no more pay for human sin in ancient Israel than a horse could pay the penalty for a murderer on death row today. What was needed was for a perfectly righteous human to willingly and voluntarily pay the death penalty for the unrighteous. The trouble, of course, was that every person who ever lived was unrighteous. Nobody could pay for their own sins, let alone the sins of anyone else.

The Old Testament sacrificial system pointed to Jesus, the perfect Lamb of God, who alone could take the punishment and guilt of sin off the shoulders of guilty men and women who looked to him in faith.

Into this utterly hopeless situation, God acted to bring hope. Jesus lived a perfect, righteous life. He had no sins for which he could die. But he did die. He died on a cross, forsaken by his disciples, suffering, bleeding and bearing the wrath of God for our sins. He was a willing, perfect and truly human substitute. His death was in our place. His death was our death. He took the sins of God's people upon himself to pay for them all, knowing that the only way justice could be satisfied was through death. Either the sinners themselves would die or their Substitute would die in their place: Jesus, the Saviour, died so we could live.

But God raised Jesus from the dead. The death of the Substitute was not the last act in the drama of redemption. The crucifixion and the resurrection—both the death and the life—of Jesus were, and are, necessary for salvation. Notice how both come together in Peter's letter. He says that we have been bought by Christ's precious blood and we belong to God. Our sins are taken away and our spiritual debts are paid in full. Moreover, Jesus, who died in our place, has defeated death! He has been resurrected to glory. He will not—indeed, cannot—die again. In God's grace and plan of salvation, all those who are given new birth and place their faith in Jesus are united with him in his life, death and resurrection. Because Jesus paid for our sins we will never pay for them ourselves. Because Jesus died yet lives forevermore, even though we die physically, we, too, will live forever and ever. By the mercy of God, this is the new, eternal life into which we are born.

As a result of God's grace, Jesus has paid for our sins, death cannot rob us of life and we will live in pure glory in the presence of the Lord for eternity. Since all this is true, when someone asks the believer why they still have hope in the face of persecution and suffering, the answer is not a philosophical argument for the existence of God. The answer is both much simpler and much more profound. *The answer is Jesus*.

Yes, it is necessary to explain who Jesus is and what he has done. Just pronouncing the name Jesus does not necessarily communicate very much. There is also a place for specialists to intellectually defend Christian claims with proper academic rigour. All of that notwithstanding, the simple fact remains that the hope of every Christian is not in their ability to defend their faith or in their intellectual sophistication: the hope of every Christian is in God through Jesus. I am saved by Jesus and not by my defence of the faith. Since the reason for our hope is the cross and resurrection of Jesus, any illiterate believer can give the reason for their hope just as well as the most brilliant Christian theologian or philosopher. This is because the reason for a Christian's hope does not vary from believer to believer. Even Christians who have never heard of apologetics know that the reason that they are saved and have hope is Jesus!

During one of my last visits in the hospital with Andrew Rozalowsky, we talked a little bit about 1 Peter. He was reflecting on the relationship between faith, trials, suffering and glory. I asked him if his bout with leukemia had given him a new perspective on Peter's letter. Andrew grinned and told me that he's been trained to be very careful when he reads and interprets the Bible. He pointed out that Peter is not just talking about suffering in general. He is not writing about the pain of cancer. Peter is writing to people who are suffering specifically for their faith in Jesus. In other words, since cancer afflicts both the righteous and unrighteous, suffering with cancer is not the same as suffering for faith. Nevertheless, it is true that suffering through cancer is different when you have Jesus. Since cancer can't take away a Christian's hope, a believer can experience the ravages of the disease with an undefeated, confident joy.

The same is true of other trials and painful experiences. No matter what we face, nothing can rob us of our hope in the Lord. This is why 1 Peter 3:15 can be applied in a wide variety of circumstances. The reason for our hope is always Jesus, but the circumstances in which we testify about him can be extremely diverse. For Andrew, his fight with cancer is what caused people to notice that he had incredible strength and unwavering hope. For many, his hope was inexplicable and incomprehensible. When people asked him how he was doing, he would honestly tell them that he was fine, all because of Jesus Christ. That was the right thing to say—after all, it's the truth.

A growing knowledge of the gospel of Christ

At this point I want to suggest that 1 Peter 3:15 is envisioning a defence of the faith that is theological and biblical more than philosophical. In other words, I don't think Peter is encouraging his audience to go out and study Epicureanism and Stoicism and proto-Gnosticism and Aristotelian philosophy and all the rest. He certainly didn't expect them to formulate abstract arguments for the existence of God. What he did expect was that they would grow in their knowledge of the gospel of Jesus Christ. When someone asked them the reason for their hope they should be able to share about the necessity of Christ's death on the cross as an atoning sacrifice. They should understand why Jesus died and why he was raised from the dead. In terms of proof, I think Peter would encourage believers to understand the Scriptures and to be able to show how the gospel is organically related to the rest of God's Word. Naturally, different believers with different gifts and abilities would do this at different levels of sophistication.

In my judgement, Andrew's reflection on the ninth anniversary of his conversion is the type of deeper, biblical-theological reason for hope that Peter was encouraging. It is not too difficult to understand that the person of Jesus and his triumphal work are always the grounds for our living hope, but they have an unfathomable depth to be explored. As Andrew said so beautifully, repentant sinners are renewed in heart. Made free. Justified. Redeemed. Adopted. Given the Spirit. Born again into new life, a new kingdom, to follow Jesus, and to be disgusted by sin. These reflections come from simply digging down a little deeper into what Jesus has done for us, and the gifts God graciously and lavishly gives to his children.

For a Christian, reading Andrew's brief reflection on salvation completely turns the inquirer's question upside down and inside out. Rather than asking how it's possible *to have hope*, it seems the real question would be how it would be possible for a Christian *not to have hope*! When a believer reflects on all the sure blessings that are theirs through the gospel of Jesus Christ, hopelessness evaporates. Not every experience in this life is pleasant, and some things hurt immensely (more than I can know or say). But to lose hope? The only way to lose hope would be to lose Jesus, and he holds us too tightly to allow that to happen. In frailty and weakness we might go through times of despair and turmoil, but in the end our hope remains. The reason for our hope is not sunny skies, cancer-free bodies, ninety years of life or a good retirement plan. It is Jesus. Jesus, Jesus, Jesus. And when people ask the reason for our hope—no matter what the circumstances—Jesus is the one we must tell them about.

CHAPTER 1: SUMMARY AND APPLICATION

REMEMBER

> Praise be to the God and Father of our Lord Jesus Christ! In his great mercy he has given us new birth into a living hope through the resurrection of Jesus Christ from the dead, and into an inheritance that can never perish, spoil or fade. This inheritance is kept in heaven for you, who through faith are shielded by God's power until the coming of the salvation that is ready to be revealed in the last time (1 Peter 1:3–5).

REFLECT

1. Only the Holy Spirit can grant life transformation. In fact, Christianity is so radical it is called the *new birth* or *new creation* (John 3: 3,7; 2 Corinthians 5:17). What priority should we then give to prayer and the Holy Spirit's role before declaring and defending the faith? What comfort and confidence does the Holy Spirit bring?

2. How did Andrew's hope transcend his present circumstances? Does your hope transcend your current trials and challenges in life? If so, how? How would you counsel others going through the minefields of life?

3. "Believers are not to expect that they will be exempted from trials: they are expected—and empowered—to rejoice through them." How would you explain this statement to believers and seekers?

REJOICE

John Newton (1725–1807) was a preacher and former slave-ship master. These verses are from "Amazing Grace," one of his most well-known hymns.

Amazing grace! How sweet the sound
   That saved a wretch like me!
I once was lost, but now am found;
   Was blind, but now I see.

Through many dangers, toils and snares,
   I have already come;
'Tis grace hath brought me safe thus far,
   And grace will lead me home.

Yea, when this flesh and heart shall fail,
   And mortal life shall cease,
I shall possess, within the veil,
   A life of joy and peace.

—*John Newton (1779)*

2

What is the Christian worldview?

When we tell people that the reason for our hope is Jesus Christ, more often than not we will need to elaborate. Many people today reject the Bible, even though they do not know anything about it. They do not understand the significance of sin, why Jesus died or how his death relates to them. We cannot assume that people have even a basic grasp of Christian doctrine or the content of the Bible. Actually, a lot of people have so many muddled misunderstandings of the nature of Christianity that we have to spend time clarifying what we actually believe. This alone can prove to be a very helpful defence of the faith, since a number of people have rejected a caricature of Christianity rather than the real thing. Any defence of the gospel is naturally going to have to defend the *gospel itself*. As a result, being able to explain the gospel to those who don't know what it is (even if they think they do) is often the first step in defending the faith.

Imagine you are talking with a skeptical friend. You have mutual respect for each other and a good relationship, so the conversation is not antagonistic or about scoring debating points. Your friend has taken the time to understand the gospel and can accurately explain core Christian doctrines. They can even quote some key Bible passages you have given them. Far from being a persecutor—or even insulting—they are genuinely warm and kind. Nevertheless, they remain skeptical that Christianity is true. What kinds of issues and questions might they bring up? Perhaps your friend respects your personal faith, but they just aren't sure that God exists, so they ask you how you know that God is real. They might want to know if there is any evidence for the claim that Jesus was resurrected from the dead. Maybe they are very sensitive and cannot understand how a good, all-powerful God could allow so much pain and suffering in the world. It is also possible that they might grant you that your faith in God will bring you to heaven, but they believe that all religions are equally valid. The list of possible issues is endless.

No matter what questions are raised, you must not forget that your hope is in Jesus. But your friend already knows that. They know the story of Jesus' life, death and resurrection. They understand, in theory, the necessity of Christ's substitutionary atonement for sinners. What they want to know, however, is *why* they should believe it. In other words, they want to know what rational grounds exist for accepting the claims of the gospel. Your friend might agree that it would be nice if the gospel were true, but they don't want to believe something on the ground that it's nice or convenient: truth, not nicety, is what commands their assent. We need to be clear that Jesus is the reason for our hope, but once most people know this, there will still be many issues they want to discuss.

When we respond to follow-up questions, we are engaging in the contemporary discipline of Christian apologetics. As anyone who has been active in defending the faith knows, follow-up questions tend to lead to more follow-up questions. Rational investigation and conversation is often a fairly riotous activity when humans are involved. Our discussions often follow unpredictable twists and turns. How many times have you paused in the middle of a good conversation and asked, "How did we end up on *that* topic?" The number of pathways a discussion can branch into is virtually limitless. No two conversations will ever be identical. This means that discussing the faith is as much an art as a science. It also means that we need to learn how to *listen*.

I remember being very disappointed the first time I listened to a series of lectures by a world-renowned Christian apologist. It was my first exposure to the subject of apologetics, and I was fully expecting that the course would consist of a catalogue of answers to tough questions. My assumption was that this brilliant apologist would say things like, "When a non-Christian says x, you defeat them by saying y." Nice and easy. I figured that since Christianity was true it wouldn't be difficult to defend. It also made sense to me that every intellectual move a skeptic could make would be easily countered by a knock-out argument. Now that I'm teaching apologetics I realize it's not quite that simple. Yes, there are good answers to difficult questions, but there is a lot we don't understand and a lot we don't know. People also have a knack for asking questions we've never considered and bringing up arguments and evidence we've never studied. Only by listening attentively will we know when to speak and what to say—and sometimes what we should say is, "I don't know."

THE BIG PICTURE

Since there is more to know than we'll ever learn, we have to train ourselves to keep focused on the big picture. We need to resist going down every rabbit trail and looking under every rock. In apologetic discussions, there is a constant danger of getting sidetracked. It is very easy to miss the forest for the trees. This does not imply that the conversation should lack spontaneity, or follow a prearranged script. It also doesn't mean that your friend's particular interests should be brushed aside. For example, if they're a scientist, they may have lots of questions about the relationship between faith and science. Another friend may know nothing about science but feel that every religion leads to the same place. By all means, their particular concerns and interests need to be addressed. Still, it is entirely possible to end up arguing about one leaf on one branch of one tree in the whole forest. A whole discussion can end up hijacked by one issue that, in the final analysis, isn't even very relevant.

Take, as an example, the controversy that surrounds the Roman Catholic Church's treatment of Galileo. It is true that certain secular academics wanted Galileo censored and lobbied the church against him because—among other things—Galileo held to the earth rotating around the sun rather than vice versa. It is true that it was not only

Galileo Galilei (1564-1642) was an astronomer and scientist who posited that the earth rotated around the sun (contrary to popular belief). His assertions were rejected by the Catholic Church and contemporary scientists and philosophers alike.

religious officials who rejected his reports: many scientists and philosophers did, too. But how relevant is this, really? Let's say that it was only the Catholic Church that rejected Galileo's discoveries (although that is historically false). What follows from that fact? Does it follow that Jesus did not rise from the dead? Does it follow that God does not exist? All that seems to follow is that the Roman Catholic Church—at that time in history arguably very corrupt—wronged Galileo. Make the event as bad as it could possibly be and it still does not destroy Christianity. At worst, it's a shameful anecdote, but *it's just not relevant to the truth of the New Testament*. As a Christian, I can side with Galileo and still be a devout follower of Jesus Christ. All we do is run into problems when we vigorously argue about things that are minor rather than major. Even if we convince the other person that our view of something is right, we might not have convinced them of anything important.

The same is true in the reverse direction: when a non-believer makes a point (i.e. their uncle was a pastor and he was a hypocrite), we need to calmly assess how important it is and how damaging it is to the objective Christian faith. We get into trouble when we fight tooth-and-nail over issues that don't affect the universal truth claims of Christianity. Were the Crusades morally abhorrent? I, for one, am not going to argue the contrary. But does the political-religious society in which they were launched resemble the New Testament church? More importantly, do the Crusades line up with the teachings of Jesus? I believe the Crusades, the so called "Holy Wars" (A.D. 1096–1272), were a travesty, not *in spite* of being a Christian, but *because* I am a Christian. I don't reject Jesus because of the Crusades—in fact, it is on the basis of Jesus' teachings that I reject the legitimacy of the Crusades.

We get into trouble when we fight tooth-and-nail over issues that don't affect the universal truth claims of Christianity.

THE BIG QUESTIONS

In order to avoid camping on irrelevant issues, and to keep focused on what's most important, we need to think in terms of worldviews. Our worldview is the large-scale framework in which we understand reality. It is the way we *view the world*—it is how we interpret the big picture. Everyone has a worldview, even though many people are not consciously aware of what theirs is. If we keep our focus on the worldview level, we are not likely to get bogged down in endless and irrelevant details. This does not mean that details are unimportant: it means that we need to grasp the big picture before we can understand all of its smaller components. We need the panoramic as well as the zoom, the macro-level and the micro-level. It seems, however, that many religious discussions stagnate on one or two minor issues and end up missing the heart of the matter.

> **worldview**
> *n.* large-scale framework for how to interpret the big picture.

To correct this problem, we need to learn about worldviews—our own included—and how to analyze them, articulate them and evaluate them. There are a variety of grids that scholars use to analyze worldviews, but the major points are always the same. For our purposes, we will break down worldviews into five key categories. If we keep these five elements in mind when we are defending the faith, we will be able to assess the relevancy and importance of smaller-scale issues and concerns, as well as keep the main thing the main thing.

> **Key elements of a worldview**
> How does a worldview consider the following:
> 1. God
> 2. Metaphysics
> 3. Human beings
> 4. Morality and ethics
> 5. Epistemology (knowledge)

1. God

Belief or non-belief in the existence of God is a fundamental point of division between worldviews. Atheists and Christians cannot have the same worldview. These are not, however, the only two possibilities. For example, pantheists believe that God is everything and everything is God. An atheist cannot be a pantheist, but neither can a Muslim. Islam holds to an absolute monadic Allah; Christians hold to a Trinity. For real worldview-level agreement, it is not merely a matter of believing in a supernatural being: *what you believe God is like* matters tremendously.

Absolute agreement on every miniscule theological detail, however, is not required in order to share a broad worldview commitment. For example, all true Christians share the same basic worldview, but there are a variety of opinions about micro-level issues. Some Christians believe that God exists outside of time and others believe that God exists inside of time (and some believe that he existed outside of time prior to creation and exists inside of time after creation). Some Christians believe that God wants believing parents to baptize their infants, while others insist baptism is only for those who have made their own decision to follow Christ. Examples could be multiplied. It is critical to understand, however, that these are *internal* debates that take place inside the larger Christian worldview. Some issues are simply more important than others: training yourself to discern what's most important is essential.

2. Metaphysics

This second foundational block focuses on the essence of reality. It is concerned with the true nature of things—what something actually is, or a thing's *is-ness*. This subject is also called *ontology*. In philosophy, God is often treated as one metaphysical (or ontological) object like the rest, since you can ask questions about his nature and existence, as you can for other things like whales and stars. In worldview terms, however, the existence and nature of God is so important it is best to treat it as a special category. God's existence and nature is also profoundly different from everything else. For example, God is self-existent, self-sustaining and he depends on nothing outside of himself. Everything in the entire physical universe is completely dependent on him. Thus, even if God is thought of in metaphysical terms, it must be with the recognition that his metaphysical status is categorically unique.

Key worldview-level, metaphysical issues are contained in questions like the following: What type of existence do abstract concepts and ideas have? Do mathematical truths exist apart from knowing minds? Is the physical universe all there is? How do we differentiate one object from another? What is the essential nature of this entity? Metaphysical issues can seem rather abstract, and some are, but others are both practical and vital. In our contemporary times, we find strict materialists who believe that matter is all there is, we find animists who believe that some animals, trees, stones, etc. have spirits, and we find some Hindus who believe that what appears to be the material universe doesn't exist at all—it's an illusion. These are substantial differences. So, although metaphysical discussions can get very deep and very abstract, how we answer certain metaphysical questions is an essential part of how we understand and interpret reality.

3. Human beings

When we understand the meaning of metaphysics, we see that human beings can be considered under the category of metaphysics, too. But, as with God, the way human nature is understood creates a significant divide between worldviews. Materialists believe that, like everything else, human beings are composed exclusively of matter. People do not have souls or spirits. For most materialists, human beings emerged as a result of the unguided and goalless process of biological evolution. Our existence in the universe was neither foreseen nor designed. We are a cosmic accident without any over-arching reason for our existence. When a person dies their physical body simply decomposes. There is no life or consciousness after death.

Charles Darwin (1809–1882) was a naturalist and scientist whose theory of evolution actually creates difficulty for the worldview of secular humanism.

For those who hold to reincarnation, however, life does not end at death (nor did your life begin at birth). People are stuck in a brutal cycle of birth, death and re-birth. Although in the Western World, some people seem to regard the idea of reincarnation as beautiful (after all, who doesn't want to swim in the ocean as a dolphin or soar over the mountains as an eagle?), for those who live in the Eastern World, the concept of reincarnation is agonizing. The whole goal of life is to eventually *escape* from reincarnation's horrible and painful cycle. Whether someone believes that reincarnation, is good or bad is, for our purposes, irrelevant: what is important is that those who believe in reincarnation and those who don't, have irreconcilable views of human nature. Christians believe that people are born once and die once, after which they are judged by God. This belief entails that human beings are more than physical bodies. In the end, the Christian view, the materialist view and the reincarnation view are so different that their adherents cannot share the same worldview. How a person understands the nature of human beings is, therefore, a core component of their worldview.

4. Morality and ethics

When we are considering worldviews, we must remember that people do not need to agree on every particular ethical issue in order for them to share the same worldview. Some Christians and atheists share a common commitment to pacifism, whereas other Christians and atheists believe that there are circumstances in which it is morally acceptable to wage war. Some secular humanists believe that pornography is harmless; others believe it is dehumanizing and exploitive. There are some particular issues, however, that do reveal fundamental worldview differences. For example, Christians believe that the highest ethical duty in the world is to glorify God and love him supremely. Needless to say, there aren't too many atheists who concur.

In worldview terms, we need to think about the nature of morality itself, more than about individual ethical issues. One big difference would be whether morality is objective or subjective. Is there a universal standard for right and wrong that applies to everyone at all times? Are all moral standards simply community guidelines that are, in the final analysis, arbitrary and non-binding? Is morality discovered in the commands of God in the Bible, or are those commands to be evaluated and judged on the basis of the ethical sensibilities of the reader? Does morality even exist in the universe or are ethical judgements really just expressions of our particular emotional preferences and tastes?

There is a lot more to morality and ethics than debating the latest hot-button issues. Some people deny that morality is universally binding, whereas others reject the whole concept of morality. The former group holds that all morality is *relative*, while the latter group believes that the very idea of serious moral discourse rests on a profound misunderstanding of reality. In stark contrast, Christians believe that morality is objectively real. They maintain that God has given ethical decrees that are to be obeyed and moral principles that are to be followed.

Applying ethical principles is challenging, and there are tough cases where even people who share the same broad worldview come to different conclusions about what should be done. Furthermore, over time many people come to refine their previous views, sometimes even coming to very different conclusions than they held originally. This ethical development can take place inside of the same, basic worldview framework. Worldviews can be separated on the basis of *meta-ethics* (i.e. the overarching nature of ethics), so this should be the focus of worldview discussions. It is also very helpful to acknowledge the diversity of ethical opinions that exist inside of a shared worldview. To be a Christian, one does not need to be a pacifist, nor does one need to be an advocate of just war theory. Since this is the case, debating your personal view of war, for example, needs to be demarcated as a *sub-issue* that is irrelevant to believing in Christ.

5. Epistemology

In the language of philosophy, the subject that deals with knowledge is called *epistemology*. What can be known? Is there truth? Are some methods of investigation better than others for discovering truth? What is the difference between *knowing* something and *believing* something? Even if we know certain things, can we know that we know them? How can I be intellectually and rationally justified in holding the beliefs I have? Are all intellectual views merely a matter of relativistic perspective, entailing that all beliefs are equally true or false? Should we be radical skeptics? Is what we call "truth" really just a disguise for maintaining convenient beliefs to secure power and control?

It is not much of an overstatement to suggest that contemporary philosophy is obsessed with epistemological issues. The technical debates are extraordinarily complex. Most of the people with whom you discuss your faith, however, are not going to be specialists in this field! You do not need to master the subject to be able to identify a few key points. For example, sometimes you will hear someone asserting that you cannot know anything for sure (which is surely a self-defeating opinion if ever there was one). There are others who maintain that the only things we can know for sure are learned through the scientific method. For them, human knowledge is legitimate when it is scientifically obtained, but all other knowledge claims (i.e. about morality or God) are illegitimate. On the other side of the spectrum, some insist that humans were designed to know God, and it is through his revelation that we can have confidence in our knowledge. These options are mutually exclusive. As a result, issues of epistemology divide worldviews from one another.

THE CHRISTIAN WORLDVIEW

In the next chapter we will break down and analyze one of the most common worldviews in the Western World, secular humanism. Before doing that, however, it will be helpful to sketch what the Christian worldview says about each of the five key elements. We need to insist that the reason for our hope is Jesus Christ, and we need to ensure that people understand what the gospel actually is, yet we also need to show the cogency of the biblical worldview. Actually, we should go further: we should endeavour to demonstrate that the biblical worldview is the *only* worldview that is compelling and coherent. All other worldviews besides the Christian one fail at one point or another. More will be said about this in the following chapters. For now, however, we will turn our attention to sketching out the contours of the Christian worldview in terms of God, metaphysics, human beings, ethics and epistemology.

1. God

In regards to the first major element, perhaps it can go without saying that Christians believe in the existence of God. It is desperately important, however, to make sure that people have a rough understanding of what that means. The Christian God is not a generic supreme being who created the world and then stands idly by watching history unfold. Neither is he a benignly benevolent, grandfather-like deity who just wants us to play nice in our earthly nursery before bringing us to live with him in heaven. The God revealed in Scripture is mighty and majestic, sovereign and perfect in power, knowledge, wisdom and being. He is moral flawlessness and radiant righteous goodness. He is both high above us and intimately close to us.

There is no one like God. He is the only being that is self-existent, self-sufficient and dependent on nothing. God is holy. He is spirit. He is triune (i.e. one nature instantiated in three centres of personality or personhood, absolute unity in diversity, the One and the Many). Although there is much more that could be added, there is even more to God than we can imagine, or will ever know. He is infinite, and therefore we can never exhaustively fathom his nature.

2. Metaphysics

Since only God is self-existent, it follows that the physical universe ultimately depends on him for its existence. In terms of metaphysics, then, God is the independent Creator of the universe. He envisioned it in his mind and brought it into existence by the power of his will. Matter does not exist eternally or independently. Material reality is not the deepest level of reality. Before there is matter, there is mind and spirit. The natural laws that regulate the material universe and all physical interactions are designed and established by God. Scientists can study physical interactions inside of this order, but the very existence of this physical reality and the laws by which it operates are dependent on the mind, will and power of God.

A biblically-informed worldview understands that the physical universe is created by God. According to Christianity, the most important thing to understand about the universe is that it is *creation*. It is not eternal, nor a brute fact, nor something that happened to pop into existence one dreary afternoon. No, the universe is creation. This metaphysical system is the handiwork of God. It reveals his power and glory. It is stamped with his *imprimatur*. Every star and every microbe, every blade of grass and every supernova, from the smallest sub-atomic particle to the universe as a whole, top to bottom, front to back, side to side: it has all been created. Metaphysics is really the study of what God has made.

3. Human beings

The sheer diversity of created entities is staggering, but one of the very incredible things that God has created is you. Human beings were the climax of his creative work on the earth. So the third key component of a worldview—human nature—also receives attention in the Bible. Humans are not here on earth as a result of a series of unguided, accidental events. We are not merely biological systems with no intrinsic purpose or value. We are not cosmic orphans. Although we do share much in common with the animal kingdom, there is a *qualitative* difference between human beings and all other animal species. God has given human beings the special and unique gift of a living spirit. We are physical and spiritual beings.

More than this, we are also called the image bearers of God. Precisely what this means has been debated, and we won't enter into those waters now. The main idea is not too difficult to grasp. First, God is a spirit, and he has given each of us a spirit. Second, we are self-conscious, intelligent beings with a high capacity for rational reasoning. Third, we understand the difference between right and wrong and are morally responsible for what we do. These three points naturally function together. A fourth explanation, which is in harmony with these first three points, is that in the Ancient Near East, statues bearing a king's likeness and image were often set up around a kingdom's boundaries. Wherever the king's image was found, it was a sign that the land belonged to him. Following this line of thinking, wherever God's image bearers went, they would be living signs that God was the king who ruled the land. In other words, as humans spread over the world, their very presence would be a proclamation that the world belongs to God. Perhaps all four of these points provide a composite, harmonious glimpse into what it means to bear the image of God. We are rational, responsible, physical-spiritual beings whose very existence announces the worldwide kingship of God. Being created in God's image denotes both ontology and function.

If the most fundamental truth about the universe is that it is creation, the most fundamental truth about human beings is that they are created in the image of God. However, when we look around the world today—to say nothing of looking back through human history—it seems that human beings are capable of performing incredibly cruel acts and producing a breathtaking amount of evil. How can this be, if humans really bear the image of God? How can God's image bearers be so evil and corrupt?

How can God's image bearers be so evil and corrupt?

Sadly, the biblical depiction of the human race is not only one of glorious creation in the image of God. The Bible also records the rebellion of the king's image bearers against their sovereign. Despite being warned about the consequences of rejecting his will, the first humans decided to disobey God and defiantly go their own way. As a result, they freely forfeited their original closeness with God. Instead of finding a more exhilarating way of living—as they anticipated—they died spiritually and corrupted human nature. Biblical anthropology teaches that humans are created in the image of God, but are currently labouring under the ruinous consequences of choosing to fall into sin and evil. Human beings still bear God's image, but it is horribly marred and defaced. Now instead of being characterized by righteous goodness, we are too often guilty of self-centredness and wickedness. By nature, human beings are far nobler and far more ignoble than we tend to think.

4. Morality and ethics

These considerations about goodness and wickedness link the topic of human nature with the subject of morality and ethics. The Bible takes a definite position on our fourth main worldview issue. Many people who know a little bit about Christianity tend to believe that the Bible contains lists of commands that begin with "thou shalt" or "thou shalt not" (with more of the latter than the former). In other words, most people associate the Bible with moral rules or a code of ethics. Although the Bible is about far, far more than ethics, the Scriptures do contain moral imperatives and are deeply concerned with right and wrong. Given the existence of God, morality is assumed to be real and objective. People may not like God's moral standards, but the standards exist nonetheless. It is further assumed that people everywhere in the world have a general moral sense of what is good and what is evil. Our problem is hardly ever that *we don't know* what's right, it's that *we don't want to do* what's right.

> **Key elements of a Christian worldview**
>
> 1. **God:** is self-existent, self-sufficient and dependent on nothing.
> 2. **Metaphysics:** God is the independent Creator of the universe.
> 3. **Human beings:** uniquely possess a spirit and are image-bearers of God.
> 4. **Morality and ethics:** moral standards are revealed through Scripture and human conscience.
> 5. **Epistemology:** people can have a genuine knowledge about God, themselves and the world.

From a Christian perspective, morality is rooted in the nature of God himself. It is an objective part of his character and essence. God knows the difference between good and evil, and he has revealed it to us in his Word. He has also created us with consciences that are generally in tune with the moral law. Unfortunately, we are experts at excusing our behaviour and finding ways to be the exception to the moral rules that bind everyone else. Human moral practice, therefore, is always going to be fundamentally flawed in this world. We have a disposition to evil that education cannot erase. Yet we still know that there is a profound difference between right and wrong. A biblical worldview insists that God is intrinsically moral, he has created a world where morality is important, and human beings really do know there is a categorical difference between right and wrong. The problem is not that we lack all moral knowledge, it is that we fail to do what we know we should.

5. Epistemology

Claiming that we have moral knowledge and that we know the difference between right and wrong leads us to epistemology. In order to have moral knowledge, we have to have, at the least, some knowledge in general. God is omniscient (he knows everything that can be known). God created human beings in his image, and at least part of that concept includes our faculty for understanding and our ability to reason. Since God is omniscient, it follows that knowledge is not only *possible*, it is *actual*.

Furthermore, since God knows everything, he knows how to communicate truth. He also knows how to create a world that exists objectively outside of our minds, and how to calibrate our minds and senses to this external world, so that when we interact with it we can learn about it and grow in knowledge. Even more importantly, God knows how to create us so that we can grow to know him better and better. The Bible teaches that God is truth itself and he never lies, so Christians have confidence that God will not deceive them nor create an absurd universe. Because the God of truth designed human nature and the world into which he placed us, we can trust our senses and minds, as well as accept the existence of non-relativistic truth.

IN THE BEGINNING

One of the most fascinating facts about the Scriptures—from a philosophical point of view—is that the five key elements of a worldview are all present in the first two chapters of the very first book of the Bible. As a matter of fact, the very first verse in the Bible gives us our first two major elements: "In the beginning God created the heavens and the earth."[1] Here we have the presupposition of the existence of God and a declaration about metaphysics: God created the world.

As the first chapter of Genesis unfolds, God speaks and brings a living world into being. There is a cause-and-effect relationship between his will, his verbal command, and the creation and formation of the world. The fact that God can speak and produce what he desires would

---

[1] Genesis 1:1.

be impossible without knowledge. God also decides to create human beings in his image. Here the categories of God, knowledge and metaphysics are all present, and they intersect in the creation of human beings. As a result, before the conclusion of the Bible's first chapter, we discover four of a worldview's five foundational elements.

It is tempting to argue that the first chapter of Genesis also references morality and ethics because of its use of the word "good," but this is not a sound inference. It is true that God not only creates, he *valuates* (i.e. assigns value to his work), and refers to his creation as "good." The word "good," however, in this context does not refer to ethical or moral goodness. A hammer can be a "good" hammer, but not in a moral sense. God made light and saw that it was good, but the light did not have the property of moral purity or ethical righteousness. So even though I think we can assert that Genesis 1 contains statements of value theory (certainly some type of functional or aesthetic goodness is present), I don't think we can push too hard for the presence of an explicit morality.

A stronger case for the presence of morality and ethics in the first chapter of the Bible can be made on the basis that Genesis 1:28 contains God's instructions to Adam and Eve to be fruitful and multiply and to be his stewards over the created order. Some take this as the first command in the Scriptures, which would then fall under the umbrella of command-ethics. Are these instructions, however, *ethical* instructions? It seems that they are: God is giving his human creatures a job description that is their ethical responsibility to follow. However, the ethical nature of this command becomes more apparent in subsequent Scripture. As a result, we will take the overly skeptical position that ethics are not referred to in Genesis 1.

Amazingly, within the first two chapters of the Bible, the five major areas for the biblical worldview appear in embryonic form.

How much is lost in only having four out of five key worldview elements in Genesis 1? Nothing. The fact that there are *four* is downright amazing. Not only is this the case, but God gives a clear ethical command to Adam in Genesis 2:16–17. Thus within less than two full chapters of the first book of the Bible, all the major planks for the biblical worldview appear in embryonic form. Of course, they are not fully articulated yet, and they will be developed at great length through the process of God's revelation, but still—so quickly—they are all there. And, although this should go without saying, their presence is not *ad hoc*. In other words, Genesis was written long before any philosopher ever sat down and thought about worldview systems. The pre-critical, pre-scientific, pre-Enlightenment, pre-technological Book of Genesis—in less than two chapters!—stakes out a worldview foundation at a time when nobody had ever thought about analyzing worldview foundations. Given that Genesis is concerned with theology rather than philosophy, it is astounding that everything we need for the foundations of philosophy is thrown in for free.

Only one chapter farther on in Genesis, the tragic fall of the human race into sin and the resulting spiritual separation from God is recorded. At this early juncture, we are given the key to understanding how human beings are so valuable and capable of greatness, but also so vile and capable of evil. We are a host of contradictions. The text also records, however, how even in justly punishing his fallen creatures God shows mercy and grace. He clothes them and promises them that one day the deceiving serpent will be destroyed by a descendent of the woman (Genesis 3:15). This promise is often referred to by theologians as the *protoevangelium*, the first gospel, the prototypical promise of redemption and salvation. This prophecy and promise is fulfilled by Jesus Christ.

This very brief outline of a biblically-based worldview will have to suffice for now. Describing worldviews is a necessary task if we are going to understand them, but it is not enough for accepting one and rejecting others. Merely describing competing worldviews is not the same as analyzing them. It is one thing to say, "Worldview B makes claim Z," and another thing to determine if claim Z is true or false. How do we go about adjudicating which worldviews are more persuasive than others? Is there any way we can test worldviews to see if they are true or false? Thankfully methods do exist for testing and probing the reliability and factuality of different worldviews. In the next chapter, we will turn our attention to the issue of worldview analysis, as well as examine the worldview of secular humanism as a test case.

CHAPTER 2: SUMMARY AND APPLICATION

REMEMBER

> Then God said, "Let us make mankind in our image, in our likeness, so that they may rule over the fish in the sea and the birds in the sky, over the livestock and all the wild animals, and over all the creatures that move along the ground." So God created mankind in his own image, in the image of God he created them; male and female he created them. God blessed them and said to them, "Be fruitful and increase in number; fill the earth and subdue it. Rule over the fish in the sea and the birds in the sky and over every living creature that moves on the ground" (Genesis 1:26–28).

REFLECT

1. In sharing your faith, how would you articulate the wonder and the uniqueness of God compared to false gods and futile philosophies of this age?

2. How would you respond to the challenge that there are no absolutes within the arena of morality and ethics? Read Romans 1:16–32.

3. Read and reflect on Genesis 1–3. Make careful note of the five key worldview components the writer has articulated in embryonic form. Even in the midst of God's judgement, there is grace—do you see it?

4. As an image bearer, humankind is unique, distinct in the created realm (Genesis 1:26–27). How does this truth communicate your personal uniqueness, dignity, value and self-worth?

REJOICE

Immortal, invisible, God only wise,
   In light inaccessible hid from our eyes,
Most blessèd, most glorious, the Ancient of Days,
   Almighty, victorious, thy great Name we praise.

Unresting, unhasting, and silent as light,
   Nor wanting, nor wasting, thou rulest in might;
Thy justice like mountains high soaring above
   Thy clouds which are fountains of goodness and love.

To all life thou givest — to both great and small;
   In all life thou livest, the true life of all;
We blossom and flourish as leaves on the tree,
   And wither and perish—but naught changeth thee.

Great Father of glory, pure Father of light,
   Thine angels adore thee, all veiling their sight;
All laud we would render: O help us to see
   'Tis only the splendour of light hideth thee.

—Walter C. Smith (1876)

3

How do I choose?

It is important for Christians to remember that theirs is not the only worldview that needs defending. In contemporary Western society, Christianity is often assumed to be false, and Christians are put on the defensive. What is often overlooked is that the opponent of the Christian faith is operating out of a specific worldview, too. In my experience, when non-Christians are called upon to provide a defence for their own worldview they often end up realizing that their views are not nearly as strong and rational as they had presumed. I have also found that many fair-minded skeptics can be led to acknowledge that the Christian worldview is far more intellectually respectable than they originally thought. This happens when the Christian worldview is investigated for its *internal* cogency rather than simply being written off before being given a fair hearing. Too often, Christianity is considered guilty until proven innocent (with the standard of proof being unreasonably high), while materialistic atheism is considered innocent until proven guilty. A Christian is under no obligation to accept this arrangement, nor should they. Every worldview needs to be defended.

ANALYZING WORLDVIEWS

1. Consistency

When it comes to analyzing worldviews, there are a variety of things to consider. Perhaps the best place to start is with identifying the main planks of the worldview and then checking to see if they are consistent with each other. If a worldview makes claims that are obviously contradictory then it cannot be true. Spotting contradictions, however, is not always as easy as it sounds. Most contradictions lie beneath the surface. For example, it is not too often that you will find a contradictory paragraph like the following: "I believe that the only thing that exists is matter. I am a materialist. God does not exist. There is no such thing as spirit. Ethically, I believe in divine command theory and that God has revealed his commands in the Bible, which is God's holy revelation to human beings." If spotting contradictions was this easy, philosophers would all be unemployed.

Practically speaking, the presence of contradiction or inconsistency is revealed when the entailments or implications of a worldview's claims are worked out. For example, there is a view called *scientism* that maintains that the only things we can really know are things that are empirically discovered using the scientific method. Can science demonstrate that love is morally good? No, it cannot. A strict adherent to epistemological scientism, therefore, has to reject moral claims. To be consistent, they have to hold to a worldview where human knowledge is constrained to what can be scientifically verified, and thus they have to be skeptics in regards to all moral claims.

At first glance this seems consistent on a broadly logical basis, and there does not appear to be a contradiction lying on the surface. But deeper analysis reveals the contradiction. In fact, in the realm of epistemology the position maintained by scientism is internally contradictory: it refutes or destroys itself. The epistemological claim, "The only things human beings can know are things that are subject to scientific testing," is itself a claim *that is not subject to scientific testing*. What scientific test could you devise to prove that the only things you can know are things that are scientifically testable? The epistemology of scientism—precisely because it is not discovered using the scientific method—fails the test of the epistemology of scientism. It fails to reach its own standard. A proponent of scientism holds to an epistemological position that makes it logically contradictory for them to hold to that position in the first place. So what looks like a very austere, scientifically rigorous view is actually based on bad philosophy. Far from being rational, it is contradictory and self-defeating. The contradiction isn't conveniently sitting on the surface, but when we dig down and analyze the epistemological claim, it is exposed.

> **Key to analyzing worldviews**
>
> Consider the following:
> 1. Consistency
> 2. Coherence
> 3. Scope and simplicity
> 4. Can you live with it?

The presence of contradiction or inconsistency counts negatively against a worldview, and their absence counts positively in a worldview's favour. To be acceptable, a worldview must be internally consistent in its surface claims and must continue to demonstrate logical integrity after being analyzed and scrutinized in a rigorous way. Consistency by itself is not sufficient to prove that a worldview is true, but it is a good start. More than that, deep consistency is logically necessary: a sound worldview will have to be internally consistent all the way down.

2. Coherence

Although they are often used as rough synonyms, in worldview analysis *coherence* is a stronger term than *consistency*. Consistent statements merely avoid contradicting each other. Coherent statements are mutually reinforcing.

As an example, consider the resurrection of Jesus Christ from the dead. Even an atheist should recognize that there are several biblical teachings that come together in a mutually reinforcing way. The resurrection was a miraculous act of God where he raised Jesus from the dead. Why was Jesus dead? He was dead because he died in the place of others; he paid for their sins and liberated them from spiritual slavery so they could belong to God. But to die he required a real, physical, human body—this human body is what he added to himself in the incarnation. Why was this substitutionary death necessary? It was necessary because of the character of God, his love, mercy and justice, in response to our sinful condition.

So, the resurrection is not to be thought of as merely a miracle for the sake of doing a miracle. The biblical rationale is marked by *internal coherence*. It is certainly consistent to assert that: 1. God exists; 2. Jesus died on the cross; and 3. God raised Jesus from the dead. The combination of those statements fails to generate a contradiction. But when the biblical basis for those statements is examined, we find they are not *merely* consistent, they are marked by a deep coherence. They are integrally related to each other, are mutually reinforcing and are stronger and more understandable when seen in their interrelationship.

3. Scope and simplicity

So far, we have noted that the presence of inconsistency or contradiction counts against a worldview, whereas the presence of coherence is positive. These are good starting points, but there is more to look for. Worldviews need to balance *simplicity* and *scope*. A worldview that is marked by simplicity will account for all the relevant data with the simplest explanation. It will not multiply unnecessary points as it seeks to understand and describe reality. In other words, a worldview that is marked by simplicity is as uncomplicated as possible.

Simplicity, however, must not be mistaken with oversimplification. If a complex answer is required, a simple answer will be neither helpful nor true. On the other side of the spectrum, overly complicated answers aren't any better. Answers that do not contain enough detail are insufficient, but answers that contain all kinds of superfluous and unnecessary statements are not an improvement. This is why a worldview's simplicity needs to be evaluated in conjunction with its scope. We are not just looking for a simple answer, we are looking for the simplest answer that truly accounts for all the relevant data and evidence. This can also be called *explanatory* scope, or *comprehensiveness*. A worldview should represent the simplest sufficient explanation possible.

To make the distinction clear—and to show why they are both important—think of a criminal trial. Imagine an individual who has been charged with armed bank robbery. This person has been clearly seen on bank surveillance cameras committing the crime. They are the only person recorded. Furthermore, all the money stolen from the bank was discovered hidden under their bed. It's possible that a defence lawyer could argue that their client was framed. It could be suggested that the surveillance footage was really produced by a brilliant computer programmer. Perhaps the defendant was framed as part of a great global conspiracy. Perhaps the bank president orchestrated the whole affair so they could be interviewed by the media and get some publicity. This defence does provide an explanation, but there are so many incredible details, so many unnecessary hypotheses and such a large number of unwarranted speculations that the judge would dismiss it. There is a simpler answer that covers the case: the defendant is guilty as charged.

On the other hand, imagine another legal case where someone is charged with stealing a luxury sports car from a dealership parking lot. This defendant was also recorded by surveillance cameras, but not in the act of stealing the vehicle. They were recorded earlier that morning looking at the cars, taking picture, and chatting with sales personnel. The person who was recorded in the act of stealing the car does not appear clearly enough to identify whether or not it was the defendant. Furthermore, the defendant is a teacher who was in their classroom on the other side of the city at the time the theft occurred. All of their students, several teachers and the principal can testify that the defendant was at the school. We would likely be fairly unimpressed if the prosecuting attorney stood up in court and said: "On the day the car was stolen, the defendant was recorded at the dealership taking pictures of the vehicles. One of the salespeople will testify that the defendant said they really wished they could afford to buy one of those cars. Since the defendant wanted one of the cars but could not afford to buy one legally, they came back later that day and stole the vehicle." It is doubtful this line of argumentation would be convincing.

But why does this line of reasoning fail? It does, after all, provide a simple explanation. The defendant was at the dealership, they wanted one of the cars and a car was stolen. Even though this explanation is simple, the problem, of course, is that it does not take into account the most important pieces of *evidence*. How does this case explain the testimony from the school? Do people always steal things they want but cannot afford? Does everyone who admires luxury cars end up stealing one? All the relevant facts need to be considered. The explanation must be comprehensive enough to cover all the data. We do not only look for *simple* explanations, we look for *full* explanations. Although multiplying unnecessary ideas is to be avoided, failing to deal with all the relevant evidence is just as bad. A sound worldview will provide a simple explanation that is comprehensive enough to account for all the data. Simplicity and scope go together.

> **A sound worldview will provide a simple explanation that is comprehensive enough to account for all the data.**

4. Can you live with it?

The list of criteria used to judge worldviews can become relatively lengthy. Even the categories I have mentioned can be subdivided for more precision. For our purposes, we will only need to identify one more worldview test. This one is more debatable, but it tends to exercise a tremendous amount of practical influence in daily life. It is a test that is more subjective and emotionally or existentially grounded.[1] Put simply, the test is whether or not we can live with the worldview in question.

Can someone who advocates a radical epistemological skepticism *survive*? If they were consistent, they could not: they actually cheat on their philosophy every time they make decisions about what to eat and when to cross the street. A consistent skeptic would not know if they saw a bus coming toward them or not, nor would they have a belief about what would happen to them if they stepped in front of it. This is ridiculous, and real life has a way of proving that. Despite what some people say, there isn't an absolute skeptic anywhere on the globe. More poignantly, could we live without ethical values, beauty and love? Can we really live under the constraints of a worldview that claims that moral values do not really exist and that torturing children is the moral equivalent of loving them? Does the alleged moral relativist really act that way in the course of daily life? If the principles of one worldview threaten our survival, but we find a different worldview that allows us to flourish and that dovetails with our existential situation, the latter worldview is preferable to the former. This does not mean that our feelings are to be privileged over rational analysis—but, all things being equal, we should be looking for the place where rationality and livability are united.

It is at this intersection of theory and practice, intellect and emotion, reflection and action, thinking and feeling, where beliefs and living life coalesce. In order to live well, we need cognitive rest and emotional harmony. Our beliefs should be livable both in terms of allowing us to survive in the world and in terms of underwriting a meaningful existence.

---

[1] Something that is *existential* is concerned with our human *existence*. Existentialism can refer to a school of philosophical thought, but at a broader level it simply refers to our experiences as existing beings in the world.

What countless Christians have discovered is that the Christian worldview is eminently livable. In the particular case of Andrew, Christianity was tried and proven to be sufficient for both life and death. It passes the test of live-ability, but goes even further and passes the test of die-ability: the Christian worldview provides a deeply meaningful framework for both a fully significant life and death. Furthermore, it is not merely *temporally* liveable, it is *eternally* liveable. In fact, for the Christian the expectation is that life gets better after death. Christianity transforms life, but it also transforms death, since death gives way to a higher, better, richer type of existence. This creates a tension. For an individual believer, it is better to die and be with Christ in glory, but we feel the strong desire to stay in this world for the sake of the ones we love, to help them and love them during their journey.

About six weeks before he went to be with the Lord, Andrew reflected on these truths in a blog post entitled, "To Live Is Christ, To Die Is Gain—A Reflection on the Tension." He wrote:

> *I've had to reflect hard on Paul's strong language in his letter to the Philippian church:*
>
>> *For to me, to live is Christ and to die is gain. If I am to go on living in the body, this will mean fruitful labor for me. Yet what shall I choose? I do not know! I am torn between the two: I desire to depart and be with Christ, which is better by far; but it is more necessary for you that I remain in the body. Convinced of this, I know that I will remain, and I will continue with all of you for your progress and joy in the faith, so that through my being with you again your boasting in Christ Jesus will abound on account of me (Philippians 1:21–26).*
>
> *What should I pray for as I lie in a hospital bed with leukemia? Should I pray for healing, desiring to live a long earthly life? Or, should I pray in some sense to die that I might "gain" Christ and be with him face to face?*
>
> *There is a tension, and Paul in his own situation recognized it: "I am torn between the two." I feel the tension too in my situation.*
>
> *To begin with the dying aspect, think of the gain! Done with pain*

and in the arms of Jesus. Obtaining the outcome of my salvation. So beautiful.

But I think about what I would leave behind. The hardest part of this journey so far has been the emotional turmoil of thinking about my wife losing a husband and my kids losing their dad. It churns me up inside. Ugh, their pain sends me into tears. (Paul didn't have a wife and kids!)

I think also of what God has done in my life by his wonderful grace to set my heart aflame for him. I want to have many years to share this with my family and in ministry to whoever God would be pleased to bring into my path. I want to preach and write more! I've learned so much! And I would love to keep growing over the next 30–40 years in this way.

But whereas Paul was convinced he would remain within the body for a time "for your progress and joy in the faith" I don't know that in my situation.

So, how am I going to pray in response?

> Lord, I desire above all that you would be made to look wonderful through my sickness. I desire to grow in my own knowledge and love of you. You put my sin to death and made me alive in Christ and I have no greater joy! It may be that you will get the most glory by my passing. It may be that you want to show yourself sufficient when all else is stripped away and you have done that—thank you!
>
> But I desire as well to continue on in the body (to live is Christ) to continue with my brothers and sisters for my and their progress and joy in the faith, that through my being with my family and others our boasting in Christ will abound.
>
> Father, you are in control of all things. Though this cancer is trying to kill me, you may decide otherwise. I do hope for that. But I trust your good ways; whatever the outcome.
>
> There is no greater joy than knowing you. I pray these things in Christ's name, Amen.

No matter what, his grace is sufficient and he is the joy of my heart. I and my family have hope beyond the grave because Jesus has conquered sin and death.

SECULAR HUMANISM

Now that we have briefly considered worldview-testing criteria, we will explore the worldview of *secular humanism*. Given our purpose and space, the following discussion will touch only on certain salient points and not be close to exhaustive. Nevertheless, the conclusions that are drawn are capable of being substantiated and defended at great length. Whole books can be devoted to testing a particular worldview. At present, we will have to be content with painting with a broad brush.

Before *testing* secular humanism's claims, we need to *identify* its main building blocks. Secular humanists are atheists. In terms of metaphysics, they hold to what is either called *materialism* or *naturalism* (i.e. only matter exists, not spirit; only physical nature exists, not the supernatural). Human beings are the product of unguided naturalistic evolution. Genetic mutations are naturally selected when they confer survival advantage to an organism, thus allowing it to reproduce and pass on its genetic material. The existence of human beings is owing to these processes, as is the existence of all other biological life forms. For morality and ethics, secular humanists hold to the reality of good and evil, right and wrong. They believe that human beings can do things that are genuinely moral or immoral. In regards to knowledge, secular humanists believe that human beings can know things with certainty. Exactly which technical epistemology they favour varies, but they do believe that human beings are capable of forming and holding justified true beliefs (i.e. having knowledge). To summarize, they are atheists and materialists who accept the existence of moral good and evil, as well as believe that human beings are capable of knowing a wide variety of things.[2]

> **Key elements of a secular humanist worldview**
>
> 1. **God:** does not exist (atheists).
> 2. **Metaphysics:** the universe consists solely of matter and energy.
> 3. **Human beings:** are the product of unguided naturalistic evolution.
> 4. **Morality and ethics:** good and evil, morality and immorality exist.
> 5. **Epistemology:** human beings are capable of forming and holding warranted true beliefs.

---

[2] There is, of course, a significant amount of diversity among secular humanists, just as there is a significant amount of diversity among Christians. These large building blocks, however, do characterize secular humanism as a system of thought, as any reading of the *Humanist Manifesto* or the *Humanist Manifesto II* will show.

It will be profitable at this point to look at the basic narrative that secular humanists construct to explain the world as they see it. Although there are some competing models for the origin of the universe, for a number of decades the Big Bang model has, hands down, been the preferred paradigm among scientists. What is not always appreciated about this model is that its beginning point requires the emergence of something out of nothing. The model not only packs all of the matter in the universe into an unimaginably small singularity, it actually reduces the singularity to nothingness. This means that before the existence of the singularity there was nothing. Functionally, then, the universe came into existence out of nothing.

Once the universe began to exist, however, it expanded and expanded into the way that it is today. (In fact, it is still expanding, and its rate of expansion is increasing.) Over the eons galaxies formed. Eventually, our solar system came into being. Then, one day, on the third planet from the sun, something fantastic and unimaginable occurred: dead matter was changed into living matter. This vulnerable speck of living matter not only survived destruction, it became the basis for self-replicating life. These self-replicators, through mutation, eventually morphed into the whole host of countless, diverse life forms that have ever lived on the planet. Up until now, as far we know, human beings are the most highly complex results of this naturalistic, blind process.

In the view of secular humanism, human beings are biological organisms that emerged without any purpose, design, intention or plan. They are the natural products of material particles and the laws of physics and chemical interaction. Human beings are equipped with an *emergent* consciousness: when certain elemental components combine into higher levels of complexity, *emergent* properties are the new realities that transcend the properties of the individual parts. Every cell of the brain has weight, spatial extension and molecular composition; as a result, the whole brain has weight, spatial extension and a molecular composition. Since each part of the brain has these properties, they are natural rather than emergent. For consciousness, none of the particles, molecules or cells in the brain has the property of consciousness. Actually, there isn't a single particle, molecule or cell in the entire human body that is conscious. Yet human beings have consciousness. The property of consciousness, therefore, has to be an emergent one, given naturalism.

Not only do human beings have an emergent consciousness, their consciousness is calibrated to the formation of true beliefs about themselves and the world around them: it can even reliably navigate through the realm of abstract ideas. Secular humanists are not epistemological skeptics. Neither are they moral skeptics. Not only does our emergent intelligence identify apples as edible, it also allows us to know that unnecessarily inflicting extreme pain on people is morally reprehensible. The case involving the apple and the case involving the unnecessary infliction of pain belong to entirely different spheres of philosophical discourse (the physical and the moral, respectively). It is entirely possible to know a wide variety of things about the physical world without knowing anything about morality (or even without ever thinking about morality). It is important to note, at this point, that not only does secular humanism posit an emergent consciousness, this consciousness is capable of reflecting on ethical issues and coming to the proper moral conclusion.

Analyzing secular humanism
1. Everything from nothing
Although much more could be said, we are now in a position to perform a preliminary analysis of this worldview. We will begin, naturally enough, at the beginning. Recall that the Big Bang model requires that all the matter in the universe be collapsed back into a vanishingly small singularity. One step further back, and this singularity vanishes into nothingness. Literally nothing. In my judgement, the old philosophical principle *ex nihilo nihil fit* (i.e. "out of nothing, nothing comes," or "nothing comes out of nothing") is as certain a metaphysical axiom as is likely to ever be found. How was the entire universe produced out of nothing?

When we think of absolute nothingness we tend to think of a field of blackness. But this is not what nothing is. Nothing (no-thing) has no properties or characteristics. It has no power or ability to do or effect any-thing. In all of their other reasoning, scientists and philosophers have no problem accepting this axiom. Nobody believes that when something happens in a lab, it was caused by nothing. Nobody believes that nothing is responsible for keeping our feet firmly on the surface of the earth. Nobody believes that nothing has ever produced anything. Unless, of course, you are a scientist or philosopher who believes without evidence that nothing produced the entire universe. Christians believe that before God created the universe *Ex nihilo* (i.e. out of nothing), there was nothing besides himself. Secular humanists believe that nothing created the universe out of nothing. I think that if we actually come to understand what nothing is (there is nothing that it is, of course), we will realize that it is logically impossible for something or any-thing to come out of it. But, for the sake of argument, I will modify the strength of that position and suggest that, at a minimum, it seems irrational to believe that anything—let alone everything—has come out of nothing.

Secular humanists believe that nothing created the universe out of nothing.

Secular humanism doesn't appear to be off to a very promising start. Against everything in human experience and in violation of a well-pedigreed philosophical axiom, we have a universe that came into existence—for no reason, because nothing is neither intentional nor intelligent—out of nothing. What kind of universe would we expect this to be? This may seem like an odd question, because it would seem impossible to say what kind of thing would causelessly pop out of nothing. But according to secular humanists, not only did one thing emerge out of nothing, this one thing happened to be a singularity which contained all the elements and laws of the entire universe as we know it. Of all the things that could come out of nothing, surely this one is extraordinarily impressive!

If one decided to playfully ignore their entire experience, perhaps one could imagine a single particle popping into existence—but all the matter in the universe? The one thing that came out of nothing *was not less than the entire universe*? And what a universe! This is not a small place, or a random place: it is a cosmos, not a chaos. There are huge amounts of matter, precisely balanced quantities of different particles, the perfect blend of laws, force, and constants governing physical, electrical and chemical interactions, and all of these unfathomably perfect requirements for a life-producing universe apparently came out of nothing for no reason.

Remember, since nothing has no power nor intelligence, there is no reason why some particular thing has to come out of it (even if such an idea isn't simply impossible). Why should our universe be governed by laws which allow for life, or have the necessary constituent chemicals

How do I choose? 51

and rules governing their interaction to be life-producing and life-sustaining? To believe that *some-thing* came into existence out of nothing seems irrational. To believe that *this universe* came into existence out of nothing is indescribable.

Secular humanism's plausibility is not increasing. Not only is there literally no reason to believe that something can come from nothing—and plenty of good reasons to think it's impossible—there is also nothing that would make our universe have any particular constitution. Science can describe the physical laws that operate in our universe, but science cannot explain *why* our universe has these laws in the first place. Einstein famously remarked that the most incomprehensible thing about the universe is that it is comprehensible. Why should it be comprehensible? How could it even exist? Why should the universe be governed by laws instead of being a pure chaos? More searchingly, why is the something that came from nothing calibrated to be the home of accidentally generated intelligent, moral observers?

2. Astronomical improbability

Stephen Hawking (1942–) is a British theoretical physicist and cosmologist.

Even if we bypass the logical principle of *ex nihilo nihil fit*, there are also scientific reasons to believe that there is something—instead of nothing—behind the universe. The very fact that the Big Bang resulted in our universe is mind-bogglingly improbable. Famed scientist Stephen Hawking calculates: "If the rate of expansion one second after the big bang had been smaller by even one part in a hundred thousand million, million, the universe would have recollapsed before it ever reached its present size. On the other hand, if the expansion rate at one second had been larger by the same amount, the universe would have expanded so much that it would be effectively empty now."[3] This statistic is beyond human comprehension. The number can be written down, but it is so astronomically large our minds cannot grasp its meaning.

---

[3] Cited in Douglas Groothuis, *Christian Apologetics: A Comprehensive Case for Biblical Faith* (Downers Grove: IVP, 2011), 250.

We will try, however, to reflect a little bit on the implications of this statistic. Notice the absolute precision. The singularity comes into existence out of nothing, for no reason, and then there is a Big Bang . (What caused it has never been specified scientifically, it simply happened.) Now, one second after this event, if the rate of expansion was merely *one* part higher or *one* part lower in a hundred thousand million, million, then our universe would not exist. Move an infinitesimal fraction one way or the other and there is no possibility of life in the universe. Given naturalism, this is a staggering fact: without any purpose, plan, reason or guidance, the universe came from nothing and expanded in the only range—no variation tolerated by more than one part in a hundred thousand million, million—that could provide even *the possibility* of life, let alone turn out to be a place where life would *actually emerge, survive and flourish.*

On top of the philosophical difficulty of something coming from nothing, and the incomprehensible odds against the universe being potentially inhabitable, there are more enormously improbable events that must occur for life to appear. All the chemical interactions must be just right; all the molecular structures must harmonize. There must be proper ratios of elements, and all the forces in the universe (i.e. gravity, magnetism, etc.) must be perfectly balanced. Given naturalism, there is no underlying reason why any of these things should have the parameters they do. There is simply no rational explanation for why the universe should be life-permitting, life-producing and life-sustaining.

There is simply no rational explanation for why the universe should be life-permitting, life-producing and life-sustaining.

Not only is this the case, but even if a universe has the necessary calibration to be potentially life-permitting, this does not mean that the odds of life being found in it will be high. It only means that the odds of life existing in the universe is greater than zero. It in no way indicates that the existence of life is probable or expected. All we have done in finding a life-permitting universe is find a universe where the existence of life is not a flat-out impossibility.

On the popular level, it is often urged that evolution provides a complete explanation for the existence of human life. This is patently false (and no serious scholar suggests it's true), because evolution deals with the origins of *species*, not the origins of *life itself*. The theory of evolution states that positive genetic mutations give an organism a new adaptive advantage, which in turn raises the odds of its being able to survive and reproduce. As a result, the strongest organisms survive and reproduce ("survival of the fittest"), passing on their genetic material. The beneficial adaptations allow for biological descent with modification. Through long ages of time and astronomical numbers of unguided, beneficial mutations—positive, not negative, mutations—life evolves into greater complexity and diversity.

One of the features of this model that is sometimes overlooked is that the process of evolution cannot possibly begin unless living matter *already exists*. More to the point, this pre-existing living matter must be capable of *self-replicating*. In order to reproduce, genetic material must replicate itself. Evolution is not a force: it is a description of a process. Unless there is pre-existing, self-replicating, living genetic material, there cannot be evolution: the evolutionary process has no independent existence. In other words, evolution cannot provide a full account for the existence of human life because evolution cannot account for the *existence of life* in the first place. What is required is the emergence of life from dead matter, and evolution is completely irrelevant to this phenomenon.

Although there have been different experiments that have attempted to demonstrate how dead matter on our planet could begin to live, none has been successful. In fact, Francis Crick, the co-discoverer of DNA's double-helix structure, argued that, given the planet's physical environment, it was impossible for life to begin here on earth. As an alternative, he proposed a hypothesis called "directed panspermia." According to this theory, life began somewhere other than earth, evolved, and then was purposefully sent to earth by super-intelligent aliens. Once the basic living matter was on this planet, evolutionary processes led to the formation of complex life-forms. Crick's scientific credentials are impeccable, and he is a religious skeptic. Even though there is not one shred of evidence to support his panspermia hypothesis, as a scientist he knows that in a naturalistic system, it was impossible for life to begin on this planet.

Ignoring the way things actually were, we will suppose that the early conditions on this planet did not make it impossible for dead matter to be spontaneously transformed into living matter. Granting that it wasn't impossible, do we have any reason to think that it would be *probable*? Whether or not you accept the naturalistic account, the odds against it are staggeringly improbable. Cells with any level of complexity require approximately 400 proteins. One protein needs approximately 1,500 DNA letters. DNA contains information. In fact, it contains more information than our most sophisticated computers. Every one of these 1,500 letters has to be in exactly the right sequence. On the basis of chance (i.e. an unguided, random process), the odds of assembling one functioning protein is practically nil. To understand the odds, you need to write a number that begins with 1 and has 125 zeroes after it. That number is incomprehensible to our minds. Then you need to note that the odds are 1 in *that* number. This is not one in a million, nor even close to one in a trillion. The word "improbable" does not do justice to these kind of odds. In fact, it is more accurately described as mathematically impossible.[4]

In the narrative of secular humanism, not only did living matter spontaneously emerge from dead matter on our planet (or somewhere else in the universe before being sent here), but this living matter *survived*. We tend to take the survival of life for granted, but it is actually a very amazing thing to consider. One can only imagine that if dead matter began to live, the odds of it surviving in an inhospitable and uncontrolled environment would be appallingly low. What would prevent it from breaking down, malfunctioning or being destroyed? Why should it work so well and have an inherent property that provided for self-replication? Why should it exist long enough to replicate? In the earliest stages of life on this planet, it would only have taken one accident to destroy all the living matter on the globe. If this living matter was destroyed—or simply failed to replicate—then the world, again, would consist of dead matter alone. Therefore, to the mathematical impossibility of life beginning on this planet, we have to add the improbability of the first living matter self-assembling, surviving and self-replicating.

---

[4] *Mathematical* impossibility is not identical to *logical* impossibility. Mathematical impossibility means that the odds against something occurring are so inconceivably vast that realistically it could never happen.

3. Intelligent matter?

In order to follow secular humanism's worldview narrative, we will grant that dead matter began to live, survived, self-replicated and then grew through mutation into more and more complex organisms. The world is full of chemicals that are interacting with chemicals, genes that are cooperating and competing, chemical-biological systems that are busy reproducing and passing on their genetic code (sometimes with helpful mutations that confer survival advantage), all determined by inexplicably existing natural forces and laws. These processes continued for eons until, one day, matter becomes *aware* of its own existence. A collection of interacting chemicals becomes self-conscious. Out of non-sentient matter emerged sentience; non-intelligent matter became intelligent. Emerging from a chemical object comes a first-person ego, a subject, an "I."

This is not to say that naturalism posits a fully-formed human consciousness spontaneously popping into existence one afternoon (after all, something can't come from nothing). But no matter how humble its first state, a totally new *category* of existence allegedly came into being. Given naturalism, there is no mind behind the universe, no purpose guiding the universe and no consciousness in the universe for billions of years after the Big Bang. Not one piece of matter in the universe has the property of consciousness. Particles, molecules, chemicals, laws of physics—all of these things are non-conscious. For billions of years absolutely everything in the universe was non-sentient and there was no consciousness anywhere. Nothing was rational or irrational: everything was arational. Yet, according to the humanist narrative, over time non-sentient, non-conscious, arational bits of matter kept running into each other, and out of their collisions and reactions *self-conscious, intelligent, rational minds were created.*

It is important to understand that nobody knows how this apparently happened, nor are there any reasonable explanatory hypotheses.

> **According to the humanist narrative, over time non-sentient, non-conscious, arational bits of matter kept running into each other, and out of their collisions and reactions self-conscious, intelligent, rational minds were created.**

As a matter of fact, Sam Harris, one of the most celebrated opponents of religion and one of atheism's most strident defenders, says: "It is true that we do not understand how consciousness emerges from the unconscious activity of neural networks—or even how it *could* emerge."[5] Notice that the problem is much deeper than not knowing how consciousness emerged: it is a matter of not knowing how such an event is even possible. One of the reasons for this difficulty is that consciousness is categorically different from everything else in the universe. How can the collisions of mindless matter create minds? It is easy to say, "there is a connection between brains and consciousness, so brains are responsible for consciousness," (this is a statement of relationship), and entirely another thing to *explain* how this lump of chemical-electrical interactions became self-conscious and brilliant in the first place.

If your brain is nothing but molecules in motion, then it follows natural laws. As such, the behaviour of your brain is completely determined by non-rational physical laws. What you think, therefore, is determined by the physical laws that govern the universe. The chemical interactions in your brain are no more intelligent than the chemical interactions in a scientific experiment. If your thinking is nothing more than the production of blind chemical and molecular interactions that are only obeying physical laws (i.e. your thinking *could not* be different than it actually is), why do you trust your thoughts? At the bottom of your thoughts, there are only chemicals and molecules that have to act in the way that they do: your thinking is nothing more than the inevitable result of a chain of physical interactions that reaches all the way back to the Big Bang. As a result, you have no reason to believe that what you think is *true*. This, in turn, means that you cannot know that your brain is what you think it is! Furthermore, in this model you could never know whether your worldview was true or false.

4. Darwin's doubt

At this juncture, we will set aside the tremendous philosophical and scientific problems that plague the idea that conscious intelligence was created by the interactions of non-sentient molecules. Instead of

---

[5] Sam Harris, *The Moral Landscape: How Science Can Determine Human Values* (New York: Free Press, 2010), 221–222; emphasis in original.

pursuing those particular difficulties, we will consider another epistemological dilemma that faces secular humanism. In the humanist model, the human brain is the product of an evolutionary process where positively mutated genes are passed on through reproduction. Every sense, every faculty, every part of human nature is the result of a random mutation that contributed to successful reproduction. The problem this generates for the materialist is that human consciousness, then, is not selected by a process that cares about truth: it is selected because it aids in passing on genetic material. In other words, whether or not our brains actually produce true-beliefs is irrelevant: what counts is producing beliefs that aid in reproduction.

Darwin himself expressed the difficulty that attends trusting one's own mind given an acceptance of naturalistic evolution. In a letter to William Graham on July 3, 1881, Darwin wrote: "But then with me the horrid doubt always arises whether the convictions of man's mind, which has been developed from the mind of the lower animals, are of any value or at all trustworthy. Would any one trust in the convictions of a monkey's mind, if there are any convictions in such a mind?" Given atheism and evolution, why *should* we trust the convictions and thoughts of our brains? It is interesting that Darwin never actually answers his own question—he simply moves on. But the question cannot be dodged. What logical justification do we have for trusting our brains? Darwin called it a "horrid doubt," and his concern was well grounded. What grounds do we have for trusting the convictions of a mutated monkey's mind?

It can be granted, for argument's sake, that the production of true beliefs on a local level would seem to aid in survival. If a plant is poisonous and I eat it, I'm not as likely to survive and reproduce as the person who avoids it. Likewise, if an animal is a predator, I'm more likely to survive if my brain accurately identifies it as dangerous. Although there are still some logical difficulties with this by the secular humanist's accounting, we can grant it for now. The problem that remains, however, is that there seems to be no reason why we should trust what our minds tell us concerning abstract realities. Not only is this the case, but there is a remaining problem with why our minds

Even Darwin questioned whether one could trust the convictions of a mutated monkey's mind.

should be as developed as they are. Clearly the potential for human cognition is incredible—but all this potential lay latent for hundreds of thousands of years. What selective advantage did having the potential for abstract philosophical or mathematical reflection confer in the earlier stages of human history?

Let us return for a moment to the foundational logic of Darwinism, and see how it relates to human intelligence. Our brains are the result of a process that cares nothing for truth, only for reproduction. (Of course, the process actually cares nothing for anything, since it is not an agent.) When we say that evolutionary processes only deal with gene *replication*, we must admit that they have no concern for *truth*. In fact, if false beliefs aided reproduction, then organs that deceived us— possibly in subtle ways—would be selected. Given the logic of the Darwinian process itself, what would make this unlikely? In fact, given unguided evolution, how could we possibly know if our brains were predominantly truth-producing rather than self-deceiving? How could we know if our brains produced a high or low ratio of true vs. false beliefs? Given the basis of naturalistic Darwinism, there is no reason to trust the beliefs produced by the interactions of a chemical-electrical system that is mutated for the sake of reproduction.

Furthermore, since any test for the *reliability* of our brain will ultimately rely on our *brain*, all of our tests for mental reliability and accuracy will be viciously circular. If I don't know that my brain is reliable, I can't rely on the tests my brain devises, nor do I have any grounds for accepting the results that I think the test yields. To affirm that my brain produces true beliefs I need to assume that I can rely on its deliverances—but that's the very issue being investigated! On the logic of naturalistic evolution, mutations are only selected if they aid in reproduction—truth is not the focus. Given this scenario, there is no reason to optimistically assume that our brains function to produce true beliefs. In the first place, there is no explanation for how conscious minds are created, but even gratuitously granting their *emergence*, there is no reason why, on Darwinism's own principles, we should trust that our minds function to reliably produce *true* beliefs.

Secular humanists cannot explain the fundamental nature and reality of consciousness, nor do they have any logical reason to trust their own beliefs. Since they believe that secular humanism is true, but they have no reason to think that their brains produce true beliefs, they actually have no reason to think that their worldview is true. It is irrational and unreasonable for a secular humanist to believe that secular humanism is true. (It is also irrational and unreasonable for them to think that it is false. Since they cannot trust their brains, they cannot know if their beliefs are true or false. If consistently followed, secular humanism leads to skepticism. One further implication of this is that secular humanists cannot possibly know that Christianity is false, since on their own principles they can't justify any knowledge claims.) The worldview undermines itself.

Not only is secular humanism insufficient to account for the universe philosophically, scientifically and mathematically, it also makes it impossible to account for the existence of minds, or to trust in the beliefs that those minds produce. As a result, even debating worldviews presupposes that atheism is false.

5. Matter and morality
Although morality will be discussed in subsequent chapters, it is still worth noting here that secular humanism is entirely unable to account for the existence of objective morality in the universe. The universe came from nothing, so its source was not moral. Matter colliding with matter through long stretches of time is not moral or immoral. It is amoral. When did matter colliding with matter become moral? How did a process that accidentally ended up reproducing genetic material somehow produce moral beings out of amoral component parts? To bring back the epistemological problem of the reliability of our brains, why should we believe that our brains are calibrated by evolution to make proper moral judgements? Why should eternal moral principles just so happen to luckily aid the survival of the human race? All materialists should, at a minimum, be profoundly skeptical of their moral judgements and ethical positions.

The insufficiency of secular humanism
We will look more carefully at these issues later. For now it will suffice to review. It is astounding to think that dead matter that is mindlessly interacting with dead matter would produce living matter. For living, chemically based organisms to self-assemble and self-replicate is unbelievably improbable (if even possible). But for genes to mutate and replicate and become self-conscious, intelligent and moral—when

they are embedded in a universe that sprung into existence out of nothing for no reason—accepting this narrative is a triumph of faith over reason. It requires an unshakeable pre-commitment to materialism. Parts of the model are impossible, parts are astronomically improbable, parts are absolutely inexplicable, parts are internally inconsistent, but the secular humanist insists *it must be true*. Given these multiple problems, one is entitled to wonder what *would* convince a secular humanist to abandon their system.

Thomas Nagel is a brilliant philosopher and an atheist, but he rejects the Darwinian, materialist model because it is simply incapable of providing a sufficient account of the universe, human life and the trustworthiness of the human mind. Nagel writes, "This, then, is what a theory of everything has to explain: not only the emergence from a lifeless universe of reproducing organisms and their development by evolution to greater and greater functional complexity; not only the consciousness of some of those organisms and its central role in their lives; but also the development of consciousness into an instrument of transcendence that can grasp objective reality and objective value."[6] In Nagel's judgement, naturalism fails to provide a rational and logical accounting at every one of those points. Not only that, but a worldview system needs to account for all of these points *combined*. Secular humanism does no such thing, nor does it have the ability to successfully describe reality. Riddled with inconsistencies, improbable speculations and constructions that frankly run against the grain of the evidence, secular humanism fails to be an acceptable worldview—simply put, it is intellectually untenable.

Secular humanism is not, of course, the only worldview besides Christianity. Nor does demonstrating that secular humanism is insufficient prove that Christianity is true. Nevertheless, since secular humanism is very popular today, and some of its adherents are openly hostile to Christianity, it is important to know how unstable this system is. It serves as a perfect example of how a little probing for internal consistency, contradictions and overall explanatory power, can reveal whether a worldview is adequate or inadequate. Secular humanists often insist that Christianity is an inadequate worldview. In fact, many

---

[6] Thomas Nagel, *Mind and Cosmos: Why the Materialist Neo-Darwinian Conception of Nature Is Almost Certainly False* (New York: Oxford University Press, 2012), 85.

secular humanists believe that Christianity is extremely inconsistent. Over the next three chapters we will run some diagnostic tests on the coherence of the Christian worldview to see if they are right.

CHAPTER 3: SUMMARY AND APPLICATION

REMEMBER

> The god of this age has blinded the minds of unbelievers, so that they cannot see the light of the gospel that displays the glory of Christ, who is the image of God (2 Corinthians 4:4).

> See to it that no one takes you captive through hollow and deceptive philosophy, which depends on human tradition and the elemental spiritual forces of this world rather than on Christ (Colossians 2:8).

> Therefore, there is now no condemnation for those who are in Christ Jesus, because through Christ Jesus the law of the Spirit who gives life has set you free from the law of sin and death (Romans 8:1–2).

REFLECT

1. According to the author there are four key elements in analyzing worldviews: *consistency, coherence, scope and simplicity* and *can you live with it?* Assume you are in dialogue with a seeker, can you explain and illustrate each element in your own words?

2. How does *ex nihilo nihil fit*—a logical certainty—apply to the Big Bang Theory? Why then, in your opinion, is this theory held and propagated by so many as a support for atheism? See Romans 1:18; 2 Corinthians 4:4.

3. How does Andrew's hope compare to that of a secular humanist? How does Andrew's hope compare and contrast to the "hope" prop-

agated by *easy believism* and the *health and wealth* gospels peddled about today? In the midst of suffering, Andrew's hope was rock sure. How does this compare to your hope?

REJOICE

My hope is built on nothing less
 Than Jesus' blood and righteousness.
I dare not trust the sweetest frame,
 But wholly lean on Jesus' name.

> *On Christ the solid rock I stand,*
> *all other ground is sinking sand;*
> *all other ground is sinking sand.*

When darkness veils his lovely face,
 I rest on his unchanging grace.
In every high and stormy gale,
 My anchor holds within the veil.

His oath, his covenant, his blood
 Supports me in the whelming flood.
When all around my soul gives way,
 He then is all my hope and stay.

When he shall come with trumpet sound,
 O may I then in him be found!
Dressed in his righteousness alone,
 Faultless to stand before the throne!

—Edward Mote (1836)

Is the resurrection of Jesus credible?

"**A**nd if Christ has not been raised [from the dead], our preaching is useless and so is your faith" (1 Corinthians 15:14). This was the apostle Paul's assessment of the value of the Christian faith, if the resurrection of Jesus Christ did not really take place. In a previous chapter, we noted that Peter viewed Jesus' resurrection as the only basis for a Christian's hope. Since our faith and our hope hinge on Christ's resurrection, defending the historical reality of the resurrection is a major apologetic concern. In agreement with the apostles, we need to understand that if Jesus did not rise from the dead then our faith is useless, our hope is foolish and the Christian worldview is false.

A PHYSICAL RESURRECTION

What do Christians mean when they say that Jesus Christ was resurrected from the dead? It is essential to understand that a resurrection is a physical event. Christians throughout history have always believed that Jesus physically died, his dead body was buried and he bodily—not incorporeally—rose from the grave. Traditional Christianity has never thought of Jesus' resurrection as a vague spiritual metaphor. On the contrary, the resurrection is material and historical. Christian hope centres on Jesus Christ's physical death and physical resurrection.

It is always important to remember that the first Christians were Jews. They saw Jesus as the natural development and fulfillment of God's plan of salvation that had been revealed to Israel. They were not abandoning their religious roots. On the contrary, they were progressing up the stem to the flower. There is no debate that in Jewish theology, the concept of a resurrection always referred to the raising of physical bodies from the dead. Some Jewish sects denied that there would ever be a resurrection, but they all agreed that the idea of a resurrection involved a literal, physical event.

A spirit departing the body at death and persisting in conscious awareness did not equal a resurrection. If the physical body was not raised from the dead, a resurrection had not occurred. Technically, even the miraculous raising of the dead did not automatically constitute a resurrection. In order for a resurrection to occur the body had to be raised in a glorified way (i.e. it was a body with new properties fitted for the eternal age, not just the old body resuscitated to die again). We should say, then, that in a *technical* sense Lazarus was *raised from the dead* but not resurrected. Jesus was the first to be *resurrected* from the grave.

THE RESURRECTION IN APOLOGETICS

The resurrection is one of the most common and one of the most important issues discussed in Christian apologetics. It is also one of the most debated, even among Christian apologists.[1] This does not mean that some Christian apologists deny the resurrection actually happened. All Christians believe in the resurrection. The differences exist because there are various ways of arguing for the resurrection, and there is in-house disagreement about the value of certain arguments. Most of the discussion really revolves around the way worldviews determine what we will accept as evidence, how we will evaluate

---

[1] I treat the issues in this following section in much greater detail in Steven D. West, *Resurrection, Scripture, and Reformed Apologetics: A Test for Consistency in Theology and Apologetic Method*, McMaster Theological Studies Series (Eugene: Pickwick, 2012).

the evidence and the role that evidence plays in the construction of our worldview. For example, an atheist cannot believe that Jesus was resurrected from the dead. There are atheist philosophers who are on record saying that they cannot account for the historical evidence for the resurrection, and they cannot propose a more plausible explanation than the Christian one, but they still do not *believe* the resurrection happened. Their worldview simply precludes the *possibility* of accepting the historicity of the resurrection.

This is well understood by apologists and Christian philosophers. Some scholars believe that before we begin investigating reports of miracles, we need to determine if God exists. If God does not exist, he is clearly not performing miracles. In terms of the resurrection, if God does not exist, then he certainly does not have a Son and he certainly did not raise his Son from the dead. These scholars use philosophical arguments and evidence to try to first demonstrate that a Creator God exists, and only after that step do they attempt to make a historical-evidential case that God raised Jesus from the dead. Their goal is to demonstrate the plausibility of a *theistic* worldview, because once theism is established miracles become real possibilities. Since miracles are possibilities, they cannot be ruled out *a priori* (i.e. before an investigation of the evidence even takes place). Too often people will assert that, "miracles just don't happen." Yet, if God exists, this claim cannot be made apart from a serious consideration of the evidence for alleged miracles.

> **a priori**
> *(Latin) n.*
> **a statement that one can derive by reason alone.**

There are other Christian scholars, however, who believe that the evidence for the resurrection of Jesus Christ is so strong that the case is settled even without other philosophical arguments for theism. They would argue that since Jesus came back to life from the dead, it is clear that a miracle took place. A miracle like the resurrection could only be an act of God. Thus, a proper inquiry into the historicity of the resurrection should lead to the conclusion that Jesus was resurrected, and this in turn entails that God must exist. In this approach, the historical event of Jesus' resurrection demonstrates the existence of God; in the previous model, God's existence must be demonstrated before the resurrection can be taken as a serious possibility.

These are not the only two approaches that Christian apologists take. Others believe that God's Holy Spirit acts directly in Christians to convince them of the truth of the gospel. The gospel does not exist without the resurrection, so part of the Spirit's job is helping people know that the resurrection truly took place. As a result, Christians do not bear the burden of convincing other people that Jesus was raised from the dead (that's the Holy Spirit's job). Instead, they are responsible to defend the resurrection from the philosophical objections of skeptics who say the resurrection could not have happened. In this apologetic system, the Christian is perfectly within their intellectual rights to believe in the resurrection, even if they cannot construct a positive evidential case for its historical reality. The reason they accept the resurrection is because God exists and he convinces them of its reality. They do not prove through argument and evidence that God exists and that Jesus was raised from the dead—God convinces them directly. If a skeptic wants to argue, it is the skeptic's responsibility to prove that the resurrection did not occur, not the Christian's responsibility to prove that it did.

Another approach—which is similar in some ways—argues that the Christian worldview as a whole needs to be accepted by the power of the Holy Spirit on the basis of God's Word, the Bible. God is the highest possible authority, so when the Spirit convinces someone that the Bible is the Word of God, whatever claims it makes will be accepted. It is impossible for there to be greater proof than the testimony of God's Word.

In this approach, instead of attempting to prove that God exists or that the resurrection occurred, the whole Christian worldview is accepted as a package. When asked to defend this package, the believer suggests that their worldview and the skeptic's worldview should both be analyzed and tested with the conceptual tools used in worldview analysis. If done properly, the Christian worldview is vindicated as coherent and consistent, whereas the non-Christian worldview is exposed as insufficient. It is maintained that only the Christian worldview provides an intelligible accounting of the universe, life, ethics and knowledge. Critically, since it is only in the Christian worldview that human knowledge is possible, Christianity has to be true in order for the debate to even take place. In other words, since people can only have genuine knowledge if Christianity is true, nobody could ever know that Christianity is false. If your worldview precludes the possibility of knowledge, you can't know that your worldview is right, and you can't know that another worldview is wrong. This means that the non-Christian cannot claim that the resurrection is false—in fact, they cannot make any rational claims at all.

If this latter approach is right, then Christians do not need historical argumentation to prove that the resurrection took place. The highest authority in the world is the Word of God, and it clearly claims that Jesus was raised from the dead. Furthermore, it is not the case that having certainty about the resurrection rests on our construction of a philosophical and historical case. On the contrary, our ability to use reason and weigh evidence in the first place depends on the truth of the Christian worldview. Only in the philosophical context of Christianity does historical investigation make sense. Only in the Christian worldview can the human mind have confidence in its ability to evaluate evidence. Apart from the foundation of Christian truth, there is no justification for human thinking, reasoning or knowing. In an extremely profound sense, then, neutral historical investigation cannot prove that the resurrection happened. Rather, the resurrection is a necessary part of the only worldview that allows for rational historical investigation to proceed.

SKETCHING A HISTORICAL CASE

These reflections should not be taken as an indication that there is no *historical evidence* for the resurrection.[2] In fact, a very detailed historical case can be made that Jesus Christ died and came back to life. How this case is judged will depend on one's worldview, but oftentimes nonbelievers are quite surprised when they learn how cogent the case for the resurrection is. Without forgetting that worldviews control how we evaluate the evidence for alleged miracles, we will now sketch a brief

---

[2] Three interesting books of Christian scholarship that are worth consulting in regards to the historicity of the resurrection are Gary Habermas and Michael Licona, *The Case for the Resurrection of Jesus* (Grand Rapids: Kregel, 2004); Richard Swinburne, *The Resurrection of God Incarnate* (New York: Oxford University Press, 2003); and N.T. Wright, *The Resurrection of the Son of God* (Minneapolis: Fortress Press, 2003). Many of the ideas in the following section of this book were originally stimulated by studying the work of these authors.

outline of some of the evidence that is commonly presented in favour of the resurrection of Jesus Christ.

1. The context of the resurrection

An obvious point that is frequently overlooked is that many people in our contemporary world actually believe that Jesus was raised from the dead. Although this does not prove that the resurrection occurred, there needs to be a reasonable explanation for this phenomenon. Over a span of approximately 2,000 years, billions of people have believed that Jesus was resurrected as the Lord of all things and the conqueror of death. This belief is not waning as time advances. More people believe in the resurrection now than at any other time in the history of the world. This is an incontrovertible fact. What is the explanation for this phenomenon?

Although there are many levels at which to answer this question (theological, sociological, cultural, political, etc.), a full explanation has to track back through history to the earliest proclamation of Jesus' resurrection. For 2,000 years there has been an unbroken chain of people who accepted the reality of the resurrection and proclaimed its truth to others. How did the first link in this chain get forged (or, to shift the metaphor, why did the first domino in the chain tip over)? What accounts for the original belief and the first proclamation? How did this belief—that is now globally distributed—originate?

One of the first things to get clear is that nobody in the first century believed that people were dying and subsequently being resurrected. Unfortunately, there are scoffers today who sneer about the gullibility and naïveté of pre-scientific people (which seems to include nearly everyone except themselves). Perhaps it should go without saying that people in the first century did not understand the Theory of Relativity. (Before we get too haughty, perhaps we should remind ourselves that neither do the vast majority of people in any contemporary society anywhere on the planet. Furthermore, being able to say the words "Einstein's Theory of Relativity" does not mean that you understand it.)

If people in the first century did not have the scientific and technological knowledge that we have, what kinds of things *did* they know? Well, for one thing, they knew how babies were conceived. When Joseph discovered that Mary was pregnant he decided not to marry her because he knew what the necessary cause for a conception was. (In the first century people were at least intellectually sophisticated enough to know that something didn't come from nothing.) They knew that walking on water was a physical impossibility. Above all, they knew perfectly well that dead people stayed dead. The suggestion that people in the first century believed in the resurrection because they were fools is both rude and uninformed—it is literally ignorant in both senses of the word.

In actual fact, the message of Jesus' resurrection was completely out of step with the thought-world in which it was initially proclaimed. For the Greeks and Romans, the concept of a resurrection was absurd. Some philosophers believed that at death the atoms of the body simply separated from each other. Others, in the tradition of Plato, believed that human spirits were imprisoned in flesh and the great hope for the afterlife was that a person's spirit would be permanently set free from the prison-house of their physical body.

Plato (c.427 B.C.–347 B.C.) was a Greek philosopher. He believed that the soul was trapped in the body and needed to find release back to the eternal realm of the forms.

In the Greco-Roman context, nobody believed that the human spirit would be united with a glorified, resurrected body. The very idea was distasteful. In terms of wish-fulfillment, this was the opposite of what people wanted to experience.

Many Jews, on the other hand, did believe that the eternal state would begin with the resurrection of the body. They were anticipating that at the end of the age the dead would be resurrected to face the judgement of God. It must be understood that nobody in Judaism believed that anybody would be resurrected *before* that final day. Everyone was going to be resurrected at the same time—when God brought this era to a close and ushered in his great kingdom. The very idea of one individual being resurrected in the middle of time was bordering on nonsense, because the concept of resurrection was inseparably tied to the end times. To try to tell people steeped in Jewish theology that a resurrection had occurred in the middle of history was to try to tell them that something which they were convinced couldn't happen until the Last Day had happened now. It is difficult to overstate how theologically dissonant this message was for people living in the milieu of Jewish religious thought.

The church was born in a time and place where it was surrounded by intellectual and conceptual landscapes that regarded its central truth claim—that Jesus was resurrected—as not only untenable, but undesirable. Yet, it was in this environment that the resurrection was first proclaimed, and the message spread like wildfire. As a Christian, I attribute the meteoric rise and influence of this early gospel preaching to the Holy Spirit's work of opening hearts and minds to embrace the reality of Jesus' resurrection. It certainly cannot be attributed to a general expectation among first century people that a resurrection was going to occur, or that these people were more psychologically predisposed than we are to accept the occurrence of such an event when they heard about it. There can be no doubt that the first people proclaiming the resurrection of Jesus were Jews. What must have happened in order for them to begin believing and proclaiming that Jesus had experienced a resurrection?

The church was founded on the doctrine of the resurrection. It was not a late, developmental addition to the church's teaching. The apostle Paul wrote the earliest letters that are included in the New Testament. There is no doubt that he was the author of 1 Corinthians and that this letter was composed approximately twenty years after the crucifixion. We know that Paul was converted shortly after the beginning of the church. We also know that, after his conversion, he spent time with the other apostles. During this time, the apostles passed on to Paul a doctrinal creed that represented the church's earliest and most important teaching. Paul, in turn, passes on this doctrinal formulation in 1 Corinthians 15:3–8. There we find that *the cross and resurrection of Jesus Christ were the heart of the church's creed from the very beginning*. This is highly significant because it demonstrates that the resurrection of Jesus was a core doctrinal teaching of the church from the first day forward. Furthermore, the resurrection was being proclaimed immediately after Jesus was crucified. There was never a time in history when only the crucifixion was being proclaimed—the cross and the empty tomb were

> **... the cross and resurrection of Jesus Christ were the heart of the church's creed from the very beginning.**

always proclaimed *together*. The resurrection was not a late, legendary development that was tacked onto the church's message. In fact, apart from the resurrection, the church had no message.

2. Was it a trick?

It is a historical fact that the earliest followers of Jesus believed in the resurrection. We need to determine the cause of their belief. Something happened that generated this belief in the disciples and caused them to broadcast their message all over the known world. They announced the resurrection to pagans who thought it was ludicrous and to Jews who thought it was damnable. The doctrine of Christ's resurrection was first met with a large amount of violence and scorn. Yet the disciples did not stop preaching that Jesus was risen from the dead, and over time more and more people accepted the truth of the gospel.

There can be no reasonable doubt that the disciples were completely *sincere* in their belief. It has sometimes been suggested that the disciples stole the body of Jesus and then tried to perpetrate a great hoax for their own gain. Such an explanation is entirely insufficient. The Gospels record that the disciples were confused, scared and on the run during the crucifixion. These details are embarrassing and depict the disciples in a very bad light—there is no reason why the disciples would invent them. When people make up stories they tend to make themselves look *better* rather than *worse*. But only fifty days after the crucifixion, these same disciples are remarkably and profoundly changed. They are boldly preaching that Jesus conquered death. Even more shockingly, they are preaching in the same city where Jesus was crucified, and to the very leaders who were responsible for his death. The disciples had no reason to expect anything less than the same fate. Nevertheless, they stood up in public and preached in the name of Jesus, declaring that he was the crucified Messiah and risen Lord.

It strains the bounds of credulity to believe that the disciples thought that this message would win them favour, pleasure, power, wealth or whatever other benefits some people think motivated them. It was far more likely that they were going to be beaten up, persecuted, imprisoned or killed. (This, of course, was what happened to Jesus, and none of the disciples were foolish enough to believe that identification with Jesus was the ticket to fame and fortune.) As a matter of historical fact, over time this is exactly what they experienced. Peter Kreeft's description is memorable:

> [the disciples were] mocked, hated, sneered and jeered at, exiled, deprived of property and reputation and rights, imprisoned, whipped, tortured, clubbed to a pulp, beheaded, crucified, boiled in oil, sawed in pieces, fed to lions, and cut to ribbons by gladiators. If the miracle of the Resurrection did not really happen, then an even more incredible miracle happened: twelve Jewish fishermen invented the world's biggest lie for no reason at all and died for it with joy, as did millions of others.[3]

The disciples gained no worldly benefit from their teaching. If, for some unfathomable reason, they had decided to lie about the resurrection, it is unthinkable that none of them would have come clean when they began to experience persecution and martyrdom. What were they gaining? Is it really reasonable to believe that after being flogged and imprisoned, not one of the disciples thought, *this isn't worth it*? That when brought before their judges they would all accept the death sentence rather than acknowledge the truth that they made up the story of the resurrection? If we know anything about human psychology and self-preservation, we can be assured that the disciples persisted in their testimony only because they were absolutely convinced that Jesus had been raised from the dead.

People are willing to die fighting for all kinds of causes. Suicide bombers are convinced of the righteousness of their cause, and are willing to die to support it. Such people are *mistaken*, but they are *sincerely* mistaken. In other words, they will sacrifice everything for what they sincerely believe is true, even though it isn't. But people don't die for things they *know* are false. If the disciples invented the story of the resurrection, they obviously would not have sincerely believed that it had happened. In fact, they would have known that it hadn't. The fact that the disciples sealed their witness in their own blood proves the depth of their conviction. Something happened that caused Jesus' followers to literally stake their lives on the fact of the resurrection: What was it?

---

[3] Peter Kreeft, *Fundamentals of the Faith: Essays in Christian Apologetics* (San Francisco: Ignatius, 1988), 67–68.

Usually two points are introduced at this juncture: one is the disciples' discovery of the empty tomb, and the second is that they were convinced they had met with the risen Christ. Both of these factors must be taken together. The disciples did not believe that a ghostly apparition had appeared to them while Jesus' body was still interred in the grave. Nor did they discover that Jesus' tomb was empty and immediately run away, announcing that he had been resurrected from the dead. No, it was only when the empty tomb and the post-mortem appearances were added together that the disciples were convinced that Jesus was alive.

3. The empty tomb

Most scholars who seriously study the evidence for the resurrection—even the skeptical ones—acknowledge that the tomb was empty. If the tomb wasn't empty, the disciples would have quickly found out that Jesus' body was still buried. If they knew his body was in the grave, they would not have died proclaiming that he was risen.

But the disciples were not the only people who knew where the tomb was located. In fact, many people, both friends and foes, knew where Jesus was buried. If the tomb wasn't empty, the enemies of Jesus would have gladly shown people the truth, and the church would have met with an immediate and unceremonious demise. Rather than telling people that Jesus was still buried, however, the Jewish leaders circulated a story claiming the disciples stole the body. Note very carefully that the enemies of the church had to explain why the body wasn't in the tomb. Their explanation only made sense if the tomb was actually empty. Despite all of their differences, this was one point on which the disciples and their enemies completely agreed: Jesus' body was no longer in the tomb where it had been lain originally.

Today there has been a fair amount of pop-scholarship that asserts that the location of the tomb was unknown, or that Jesus was likely buried in a mass grave because—statistically speaking—that's where most people ended up after being crucified. Not only do these conjectures fly in the face of the actual, existing evidence for Jesus' burial, the latter operates on a flawed principle. It is completely illegitimate to argue on the basis of *general* probabilities that a well-evidenced exception has not occurred. For example, the general probability of buying the right lottery ticket is very, very small. But if you have the winning ticket, it makes no sense to throw the ticket away on the basis that it's improbable that you would have selected the winner.

General probabilities have very little to do with evaluating the evidence for *particular* events and individual situations. Granted, many people who were crucified *were* buried in mass graves. But how many of them have been worshipped by billions of people over the course of 2,000 years? How many individuals who were buried in mass graves were later proclaimed to be alive again and reigning in resurrection power? How many victims of crucifixion subsequently had friends and followers die for preaching that the crucified one was alive forevermore? Why did the Jewish leaders say, "The tomb is empty because the disciples stole the body,"[4] instead of saying, "Jesus was buried in a mass grave; of course, we don't know where the body is"? All the particular historical evidence we have indicates that the location of Jesus' tomb was known to friend and foe alike, and three days later the grave where Jesus had been buried was empty.

All the particular historical evidence indicates that the location of Jesus' tomb was known to everyone, and three days later the grave where Jesus had been buried after his crucifixion was empty.

The Gospel accounts are clear, however, that the discovery of the empty tomb was not enough by itself to convince the disciples that Jesus was alive. In fact, the empty tomb only confused them. Female followers of Jesus were the first ones at the empty tomb. They were the ones who informed the disciples (who subsequently came to investigate).[5]

On its own, the fact that *women* were the first eyewitnesses at the empty tomb is an important piece of evidence to support the reliability of the Gospel accounts. In the first century, a woman's testimony was considered far less reliable than testimony given by men. In court, the testimony of a woman was suspect at best, and inadmissible at worst. Nobody who lived in that society would invent a story where women were the first witnesses at the empty tomb—nobody, that is, who wanted to gain a hearing and have their story taken seriously. The very idea of women witnesses wouldn't have occurred to anyone—it was

---

[4] See Matthew 28:12–14.
[5] See Luke 24:1–12.

too great a violation of the society's plausibility structure. There is only one reason why the Gospel writers said that women were the first witnesses at the empty tomb: they said it because it was true.

4. *The appearances of Jesus*
By itself, the empty tomb was a necessary condition, but not a sufficient condition, for convincing the disciples that Jesus had been raised from the dead. The New Testament is clear that it was only after the disciples encountered the risen Lord that they understood that Jesus had been resurrected. Although different explanations for this phenomenon have been offered, there can be no doubt that the disciples themselves were firmly convinced that Jesus had been resurrected, and that he had appeared to them in his glorified body. Any adequate account, therefore, must provide an explanation for how the disciples—with perfect sincerity—came to hold this belief. The disciples died for maintaining that the risen Christ had appeared to them: their sincerity and conviction are unassailable. This means, therefore, that alternative theories will have to explain how the disciples came to hold a false belief about the resurrection, and why they were willing to surrender their lives rather than give up this belief.

Perhaps the most common alternative explanation is that the disciples' belief that Jesus had appeared to them was the product of vivid hallucinogenic experiences. Wracked by emotional distress, sleep deprived, longing for the fulfillment of the kingdom and not being able to cope with the loss of Jesus, the disciples hallucinated that he was alive. This convinced them—falsely—that Jesus had been raised to life. We will critique this explanation below, but for now one thing needs to be noted: Those who propose the hallucination hypothesis are acknowledging that the disciples *really did see Christ after he had died*. The question is whether the appearances were of the actual risen Christ or the product of the disciples' minds.

One of the greatest difficulties with the hallucination thesis is *the number of different people* who were convinced that Jesus had appeared to them. The disciples were not convinced by the reports of their friends. They were only convinced when Jesus appeared to them *personally*. In fact, Thomas was one of the twelve disciples, and he has been given the moniker of "doubting" because he wouldn't believe the other disciples when they said that Jesus had met with them. It is not as though Peter alone saw the risen Christ, and then all the other disciples were convinced on the basis of his testimony. All the disciples saw Jesus.

Hallucinations, like dreams, are unique to individuals. If several people are asleep they might all be dreaming, but they are not all dreaming identical dreams. Since hallucinations, like dreams, are the product of an individual brain, people have individually unique hallucinations, not shared ones. This is not what happened with the disciples. They had identical experiences at the exact same point in time—whatever the experience was, *they shared the same one.* Paul matter-of-factly states that at one time Jesus appeared to a group of 500 people—and then he mentions that many of them are still living (1 Corinthians 15:6). The only reason he mentions that many of the witnesses are still alive is because the event really happened. If you want to check the story, Paul is saying, you have plenty of people to interview.

Another problem with the hallucination thesis is that it provides no help in explaining the empty tomb. If the appearances of Jesus were hallucinogenic, his body would still be in the tomb. As soon as his enemies heard that the disciples were claiming that Jesus was alive again, they simply would have pointed out the rather inconvenient truth that the body was still buried in the grave. Any explanation for the historical growth of the church needs to account for both the empty tomb and Christ's appearances.

The hallucination thesis is a very improbable explanation for the appearances, even when considered in isolation. Its greatest weakness, however, is that it cannot be coherently related to the empty tomb in the larger historical investigation. Some skeptics try to explain either the empty tomb or the appearances, but the explanations for both need to be combined into one coherent and plausible account. It is when the hypotheses are combined—when the improbabilities are multiplied together—that we see that there is no plausible naturalistic explanation that accounts for all the data. The resurrection, on the other hand, is a simple explanation that covers all the data. Jesus' resurrection explains why the tomb was empty. Jesus' resurrection explains the appearances. This explanation, however, is one that many people are not willing to accept: not because of historical investigation or evidence, but because of their worldview.

CHRISTIANITY AND THE RESURRECTION

We also need to consider some larger worldview-level issues. It is essential not only to argue for the historical *resurrection* of Jesus, but also to argue for the historical resurrection of *Jesus*. In other words, the case for the resurrection cannot afford to exclude reflection on Jesus' identity. The Christian claim, after all, is not that God decided to show his power by raising a random individual from the dead. It is that God authenticated and vindicated his Son Jesus by resurrecting him. This means that the words and deeds of Jesus during his life are relevant for the overall case. Likewise, Jesus' place in the overarching plan of God must be considered. If God wasn't going to let Jesus stay in the grave, why didn't God prevent him from dying in the first place? Clearly, there is some massive significance behind both the death and the resurrection of Jesus in the purposes of God. What is there about the life and death of Jesus that is so unique? Why was it Jesus—as opposed to anybody else—who was the subject of the resurrection?

> ...the case for the resurrection cannot afford to exclude reflection on Jesus' identity.

This is where the worldview testing criterion of *coherence* is useful. The New Testament portrayal of Jesus Christ is more than merely non-contradictory. The individual brushstrokes complement each other and combine into a unified painting. All the stories—each deed and every word—blend into an organic whole. The presentation of Jesus in the New Testament is not only free from contradiction, all the individual contributions prove to be mutually supporting and coherent. As a result, it becomes impossible to think about the resurrection apart from the crucifixion, the crucifixion apart from the life of Jesus and the life of Jesus apart from God's redemptive plan for the world. In other words, the plausibility of the historical resurrection cannot be dissociated from its specific context, and also from wider worldview considerations.

In chapter two, we noted that the Bible claims that human beings are the image bearers of God, but fallen in sin. God is a God of perfect holiness, justice and righteousness. He is also good, compassionate, merciful, gracious and loving (more accurately, he is not simply loving, he is love). Because God is infinite, every attribute that he has is maximally perfect. He is absolute, pure love. He is white-hot, radiant glory.

He is so righteous that he cannot endure evil, sin or crime. God is perfectly good and perfectly just—this is why he cannot let the wicked go unpunished. It is no mark of goodness to let the guilty go free. Of all the words we might use to describe a judge who let child molesters and murderers go free even though he knew they were guilty, it is doubtful that *good* would be one of them. We intuitively know that genuine goodness doesn't excuse or ignore evil.

For those who persist in doing evil, the righteous character of God is a disaster. God will not sweep our sins under the carpet or pretend that they are insignificant. We are not the ones who evaluate the nature of evil: God alone knows what evil really is, because it is judged against his own perfect, moral character. The guilty cannot get a free pass. This is a moral universe because it is *God's* universe. Since every human being—without exception—is guilty before God, every human being stands justly and rightly condemned in God's court. This is nothing more nor less than justice. God giving sinners the verdict they deserve is the fairest thing in the world.

> **The divine solution is that God takes upon himself the blame for our wickedness and suffers the consequences that justice demands.**

Yet, as clearly as the Bible presents these truths, the Bible also presents God as a loving and forgiving God who is pained by his people's rebellion and sin. Even though they are guilty, God loves them and desires to restore them to a right relationship with himself. He cannot do this by ignoring their evil. Any solution must satisfy *both* his perfect justice and his infinite love and mercy. The divine solution is that God takes upon himself the blame for our wickedness and suffers the consequences that justice demands. This arrangement simultaneously upholds his justice and allows him to act mercifully toward human beings.

In taking the penalty for sin upon himself, God not only saves us from punishment but he saves us from sin *itself*. This is very important. God does even more than satisfy justice and remove our legal guilt by paying the penalty for our sin, he also restores us to a right relationship with himself—the relationship that we broke in our rebellion. Ultimately, God brings us back to himself so that we can spend eternity with him in a place that is characterized by perfect righteousness. The eternal state cannot be ruined by evil, because every human being who is there has been saved from both the penalty and the power of sin. Their nature is conformed to perfect righteousness, their desires no longer incline toward evil. They have been saved to sin no more.

There was only one way that God could take human sin upon himself and save his people: he had to become a human being. He would still be fully God, but he would add a human nature to his divine one. God took on human flesh. Theologians refer to this event as the *incarnation*, which literally means the en-fleshing of God. Full deity was combined with full humanity. Who was this God-man? Nobody in the church has answered this question more beautifully and poetically than Charles Wesley. In his hymn, "Hark! the herald angels sing," Wesley writes: "Veiled in flesh the Godhead see, hail the incarnate deity, pleased as man with men to dwell, Jesus our Emmanuel." Emmanuel means *God with us*; Jesus is our God with us.

Wesley's reference to the Godhead was a common way of referring to God in centuries past. Christians believe that God exists as a Trinity: one essential divine nature in three centres of personality, or persons. It is the second person in the Trinity—referred to as God the Son—who takes on human flesh in the incarnation. In doing so he submits himself to living a genuine human existence. He will only do what pleases God the Father in accordance with the leading of the Holy Spirit. He will live a perfect, sinless life. As a result, he does nothing wrong for which he can be punished.

Then, voluntarily and freely, he will choose to pay the penalty for the wrongs that other people have committed. Jesus can only do this because he willingly substitutes himself into the place of the guilty. The punishment they deserve is transferred to him. That punishment is death. God chose to take on human flesh so that he could die as a human being. Although Jesus never did anything wrong, he *chose* to be treated as if he himself were responsible for perpetrating all the evil in human history. The penalty for sin is death, and it is a penalty that each of us has earned and that each of us deserves. The good news is that Jesus chose to die in *our* place.

We return to our question and ask, Does God have a special reason to resurrect Jesus rather than anyone else? When put into the proper biblical and theological context, the answer is, Yes. Jesus is not a regular person who died a regular criminal's death. He is the heart and soul of God's plan of salvation in this world. Beyond this, if it wasn't for what Jesus was going to do for us, God would not have created this universe in the first place. The cross and resurrection of Jesus Christ are not only the fulcrum on which history turns, they are the *reason* why creation exists.

The cross and resurrection of Jesus Christ are not only the fulcrum on which history turns, they are the reason why creation exists.

When Jesus is resurrected he inaugurates a new era—he is the first of the resurrection harvest. More will follow. The Jews were right in their belief that the resurrection of our race would take place at the end of this age. It still will. What nobody knew, however, was that God was breaking into human history in the person of Jesus of Nazareth, and that there would be one resurrection ahead of all the others. He showed us what is to come. Jesus conquered sin and in doing so he conquered sin's penalty, death. We are called to renounce our own ways and turn back to God. Biblically, this is called *repentance*. We are summoned by God the King to trust Jesus as our Saviour and to submit to him as our Lord. Since he is Lord of all things, we do not *make* him our Lord—what we do is acknowledge who he really is and take our proper place before him. We are to entrust our entire selves to him, relying on him alone for all that we need in this world and in the life to come. This complete trust is called *faith*. Too often faith has been put forward as the opposite of reason, or faith is demeaned as the little unjustified extra that picks up where the evidence ends. Such caricatures are entirely untrue. Biblical faith is fully trusting in God through Jesus Christ by the power of the Holy Spirit—and this faith is the most rational thing in the universe.

The New Testament teaches that those who put their faith in Jesus are united with him in his death and resurrection.[6] His death for our sins is effective through faith. Jesus died for us and was raised for us. He takes on our death and in so doing unites us to his life. As he was raised to glory, those who have trusted in him will be raised to glory. Everyone who turns from their sin and puts their faith in Jesus Christ will live for all eternity in a glorified, resurrected body. Our demerit resulted in his suffering. His merit secures for us blessing after bless-

---

[6] See Romans 6:8.

ing. We have done nothing to earn the blessings we receive. The inexpressible riches of our glorious future in the presence of God are a pure, undeserved gift. They are nothing but grace.[7]

Philosophers on both sides of the debate about Jesus' resurrection agree that the case is ultimately evaluated on the basis of one's worldview, or background knowledge. Background knowledge is composed of all the other things we already accept as true. For a Christian, the existence of God is already part of their background knowledge. For a materialist, the non-existence of God is part of their mental framework. When the evidence for the resurrection is evaluated, then, it is filtered through a preconceived grid. It is impossible to weigh evidence in a completely neutral and unbiased manner. As we have seen, skeptics are not able to put together a convincing and coherent explanation for the historical data surrounding the empty tomb and the appearances of Christ to the disciples.

Christians, on the other hand, have an account that covers all the relevant data with *simplicity*. Thus, more often than not, when the resurrection is dismissed, it is not because the historical case is weak, it is because *the Christian worldview* has already been *rejected* without a trial. But why should it be? What reason do people have for dismissing the Christian worldview? There is one specific answer to this last question that is given more than any other—it is so influential that it will be the focus of the next two chapters.

---

[7] If the resurrection occurred, it is because Jesus Christ was the unique Son of God who fulfilled God's gracious plan of redemption. It shows that Jesus is unlike anyone else and that God endorses his person, his life and his teachings. As a result, if the Christian doctrine of the resurrection is true—and if it is false, then Christianity is destroyed—then it is impossible to maintain that all religions are equally valid. Wherever other religious teachings contradict the teaching of the resurrected Son of God, they must be wrong. Any claim that salvation can come through any means other than Jesus' life, death and resurrection is erroneous. The resurrection of Jesus Christ means that Christianity is true in a way that other religions are not. Full religious pluralism —where every religion is considered equally valid and true—is not a biblical option.

CHAPTER 4: SUMMARY AND APPLICATION

REMEMBER

Then he said to Thomas, "Put your finger here; see my hands. Reach out your hand and put it into my side. Stop doubting and believe."

Thomas said to him, "My Lord and my God!"

Then Jesus told him, "Because you have seen me, you have believed; blessed are those who have not seen and yet have believed" (John 20:27–29).

REFLECT

1. Reflect on the men and women who testify to the empty tomb:

    Early Sunday morning at the tomb
    Mary Magdalene and other women (Mark 16:2–8; Luke 24:1–8)
    Peter and John (Luke 24:9–12; John 20:2–10)

2. Reflect on the numerous resurrection appearances of Jesus:

    Sunday morning in the garden
    Mary Magdalene at the tomb (Mark 16:9–11; John 20:11–18)
    The other women (Matthew 28:9–10)

    Sunday afternoon on the Emmaus Road and other locations
    Cleopas and another (Mark 16:12–13; Luke 24:13–32)
    Peter (Luke 24:33–35; 1 Corinthians 15:5)

    Sunday evening in Jerusalem
    The disciples, Thomas absent (Mark 16:14; Luke 24:36–43; John 20:19–25)

    Next Sunday evening in Jerusalem
    The disciples, including Thomas (John 20:26–31; 1 Corinthians 15:5)

Sea of Galilee at breakfast
Seven of the disciples at the shore (John 21)

Mountain in Galilee (giving of the Great Commission)
Over 500 (Mark 16:15–18; Matthew 28:16–20; 1 Corinthians 15:6)

Location unspecified
James, the half-brother of Jesus (1 Corinthians 15:7)

Another time in Jerusalem (pre-Pentecost)
The disciples (Luke 24:44–49; Acts 1:3–8)

On Olivet, between Jerusalem and Bethany (this was his final appearance and ascension)
The disciples (Mark 16:19–20; Luke 24:50–53; Acts 1:9–12)

REJOICE

Low in the grave he lay—Jesus, my Saviour,
Waiting the coming day—Jesus, my Lord.

> *Up from the grave he arose;*
>   *with a mighty triumph o'er his foes;*
> *He arose a victor from the dark domain,*
>   *and he lives forever, with his saints to reign.*
> *He arose! He arose! Hallelujah! Christ arose!*

Death cannot keep its prey, Jesus my Saviour;
He tore the bars away, Jesus my Lord!

> *Up from the grave he arose;*
>   *with a mighty triumph o'er his foes;*
> *He arose a victor from the dark domain,*
>   *and he lives forever, with his saints to reign.*
> *He arose! He arose! Hallelujah! Christ arose!*

—Robert Lowry (1875)

5

Christianity's great contradiction?

Approximately two-and-a-half weeks before he died, Andrew Rozalowsky wrote these words:

> So I may be eligible for the Ottawa clinical trial for a stem cell transplant. It wouldn't proceed until the end of January so they need to keep me alive until then. I'm on oral chemo and a steroid at the moment. If that isn't helping to control/bring down my blast cell count by Friday, we're going to go another route with some different chemo and higher dose of steroids. Two ways of putting it both from my doctor's mouth: we're in no man's land and we're outside of evidence-based medicine at this point. My toe also has to fully heal (haven't talked much about that here but they cut it open last week to help a bad infection I've had) and I need to be in good shape otherwise.
>
> [My wife] Suzanne just left; we were reflecting on the hope of resurrection, the hope that all those whose trust is in Christ have. Does sickness, disease and loss suck? Absolutely. But Christ has

redeemed us from sin and its consequences so that we (again, those who trust Christ) have a true hope built on a firm foundation. That is the only reason I can be at peace right now. That is the only reason my soul is at rest. The nurses and doctors have seen it and it has started many conversations, even today. To Christ be the glory.

How is it possible to believe in God—let alone *hope* in God—when you are dying? How is it possible to believe in God—let alone *trust* God—when you are in physical pain and emotional anguish? How is it possible to believe in God—let alone *love* God—when you know your wife and two young sons may soon be left in this world without you? Doesn't the existence of evil, pain and suffering prove that God doesn't exist? Isn't the presence of tragedy, sorrow and heartbreak incompatible with the existence of an all-good, all-powerful, all-knowing God? Doesn't this represent a great contradiction inside the Christian faith, a contradiction that disqualifies Christianity from being considered as a rational worldview? Without question, people cite the existence of evil and suffering more than anything else as evidence against the existence of God.

One of the reasons this issue is so difficult is that it is not merely an intellectual conundrum or mental puzzle to be thought through and analyzed. Evil and suffering touch our deepest emotions. In fact, if you listen carefully when people discuss suffering and evil, the points they make are often based more on emotions than rational analysis. In contemporary philosophy, even atheist philosophers have conceded that the existence of God and the existence of evil are not logically contradictory. Nevertheless, evil is still taken as the strongest evidence against the existence of God. This is partly because—regardless of the conclusions that rational analysis yields—we *feel* that there is an incongruity between the existence of God and the existence of evil. People who are deeply sensitive tend to struggle more with the problem of evil than do those who are less empathetic, because sensitive people are simply more *bothered* by suffering. Being empathetic or sensitive, however, describes an emotional disposition, not an analytical one. This is not a bad thing. In fact, the world would be a much better place if we were all more sensitive to the nature and effects of evil (especially our own). But logical problems are not solved by emotions. They are solved by rational analysis.

THE LOGICAL PROBLEM

When the existence of God and the existence of evil is analyzed as a logical problem, the result is conclusive: there is no contradiction between the two. William Rowe, one of the world's leading atheist philosophers, writes:

> Some philosophers have contended that the existence of evil is *logically inconsistent* with the existence of the theistic God. No one, I think, has succeeded in establishing such an extravagant claim. Indeed…there is a fairly compelling argument for the view that the existence of evil is logically consistent with the existence of the theistic God.[1]

Rowe does not believe that God exists, but he is too intellectually rigorous to believe that the existence of evil and the existence of God are logically contradictory.

Nevertheless, countless people continue to believe that the existence of evil rules out the existence of God. People often insist passionately that they just *cannot* believe that a good, all-knowing and all-powerful Creator God would allow evil to exist in the universe. In order to bring some analytical clarity to this issue, we need to examine the logical scaffolding of the argument.

The first step is to identify the relevant characteristics of God and write them as the first premise of the argument:

1. God is all-knowing, all-powerful, and perfectly good.

The second step is to acknowledge the existence of evil and suffering. Some religions and philosophies claim that all suffering is an illusion, but Christianity squarely faces up to the reality of evil. The argument's second premise is:

2. Genuine (i.e. non-illusory) evil and suffering exist in the universe.

---

[1] William Rowe, "The Problem of Evil and Some Varieties of Atheism," in *Philosophy of Religion, Selected Readings, Third Edition*, eds. William Rowe and William Wainwright (Oxford: Oxford University Press, 1998), 242 fn 1.

It is extremely important to notice that these two premises only purport to make factual claims. The first premise makes a claim about what God is like, and the second premise makes a claim about the reality of evil and suffering. The big philosophical question is, "What is logically contradictory about these two premises?"

What is a contradiction?

Perhaps we need to ask, "What is a logical contradiction?" For something to be logically contradictory, it must be literally impossible. There can be no possible world in which all the premises are true together. If our first premise was, "God is all good" and our second premise was, "God is not all good" we would have a logical contradiction. If our first premise was, "Evil and suffering do not have genuine existence" and our second premise was, "Genuine evil and suffering exist," then we would have a logical contradiction. But our two premises are obviously not like that. They are concerned with two distinct entities and make entirely separate claims. As such, they do not obviously and directly contradict each other. It is possible that these two premises *entail* a contradiction, but nothing contradictory is immediately apparent. If we are going to find the alleged contradiction, we will have to dig deeper.

The traditional way of framing the challenge is that a good being desires to eliminate evil and suffering. Many of us would love to eradicate global poverty and ensure that every person on the planet was safe and happy. What prevents us from doing so is our finite power. If we possessed infinite power, we believe we would exercise it to put an end to all human misery. So the problem is formulated as follows: If a person is perfectly good, they *want* to get rid of evil. If they are all-powerful they have the *ability* to get rid of evil. If they are all-knowing, they know how to use their *power* to eliminate evil. But evil remains. Thus God is lacking in either goodness, power or knowledge. In other words, there is no God.

logical contradiction statement. something that is literally impossible.

Formulating the argument this way has some punch, but it is hardly the knockout blow that many atheists have assumed. As noted earlier, many contemporary atheist philosophers are acknowledging that there is no contradiction between the existence of God and the existence of evil. The reason why these premises are not contradictory is so simple that it is hard to believe it went unrecognized for so long. The existence of both God and evil does not generate a contradiction *if God has a good and morally sufficient reason for allowing evil to exist*. If it is possible for God to have a good reason for permitting the existence of evil—and the suffering that results—then the existence of evil does not rule out the existence of God, nor does it entail that he must be lacking in goodness, knowledge or power.

Moral reasoning

At this point, the big question is, what could constitute such a good and morally sufficient reason? In order to answer this question, however, we need to take a moment to reflect on how we determine whether something is morally good or bad. When we assess whether something is good or bad, what are we looking for? What principles of moral justification are we using? What ethical properties must an act, or event, or set of events, have in order to be morally justifiable?[2]

More will be said about ethical standards in the following chapters, but in terms of practical, moral reasoning, ethicists tend to fall into two major camps. The first camp believes that a given act is to be judged on the basis of the consequences that it produces. This position is, naturally enough, referred to as *consequentialism*. The second camp believes that acts are intrinsically good or bad. As a result, they maintain that an act should be judged on the basis of its *inherent moral worth*, rather than on the consequences that flow out of it. (This position can be referred to as *non-consequentialism* or *deontological ethics*. For the sake of comparing and contrasting the systems, we will use the terms "consequentialism" and "non-consequentialism.")

One quick example will make the distinction clear. A non-consequentialist may believe that telling the truth is intrinsically right. As a result, they maintain that it is *always* right to tell the truth and that there are no circumstances in which lying is ethically permissible or justifiable. To mix some clichés, the truth may hurt, but honesty is

---

[2] For the following discussion, I am indebted to the stimulating work of John Feinberg in *The Many Faces of Evil: Theological Systems and the Problems of Evil*, rev. and exp. ed. (Wheaton: Crossway, 2004).

always the best policy. A consequentialist, on the other hand, may believe that telling the truth is generally a good thing. Sometimes, however, it is possible that telling the truth could produce negative consequences. This means that truth-telling—even if generally good—is not always the best thing. As a result, a consequentialist can maintain that there are times when lying is morally acceptable.

The classic test case concerns telling the truth to someone who will use their knowledge for evil. If a person has taken refuge in your home from someone who is trying to kill them, what do you say when the would-be murderer shows up at your door and asks if their intended victim is inside? A strict non-consequentialist insists that it is never permissible to lie, so you either refuse to answer, or you tell the truth or you try to prevent the assailant from entering the home. A consequentialist can maintain, however, that since telling the truth in such circumstances would result in evil consequences that outweigh the act of lying, it is ethically permissible to deceive the individual who is trying to harm the person who is hiding in your home.

As quick as these observations have been, it is time to refocus the discussion back to the issue of the existence of God and the existence of evil. What should be apparent is that different ethicists will use different criteria when they try to evaluate whether a potential reason God may have for permitting evil is morally sufficient. Yet it should also be reasonably clear that both consequentialist and non-consequentialist views have the potential to demonstrate that the existence of God and the existence of evil are not logically contradictory. This is because a logical contradiction only exists when it is literally impossible for all the premises that are being considered together to be true at the same time and in the same way.

It is possible, therefore, for a non-consequentialist to reject consequentialism as an ethical system, but yet acknowledge that *if consequentialism is true*, God can be morally justified in permitting the existence of evil, provided that the resulting consequences outweigh the evil itself. But if we grant that there is one possible state of affairs where the existence of God and existence of evil are not logically contradictory, then we have demonstrated conclusively that a contradiction does not exist between the two. Nor do our premises entail a logical contradiction, since it is possible to uphold both premises simultaneously without violating any logical rules.

Christianity's great contradiction? 91

Since a logical contradiction necessarily involves violating one or more of the laws of logic, and since we can hold to both premises without violating any of these laws, it follows that we can hold to both the existence of God and the existence of evil in a way that is logically coherent. There is no logical contradiction between the existence of God and the existence of evil.

TWO LOGICAL POSSIBILITIES

At this point our observations have been theoretical, but some scholars have made practical proposals that endeavour to look at our world and figure out what possible reasons God might have for allowing evil to exist. Two such proposals occupy a prominent place in the literature. The first is the *free will defence* (FWD) and the second is the *greater good defence* (GGD). The GGD is consequentialist in its ethical orientation, whereas the FWD can be employed in more than one ethical framework. Since it is the FWD that has been mainly credited with demonstrating that the existence of God and the existence of evil are not logically contradictory, we will examine it first.[3]

1. The free will defence

The FWD maintains that although God is all-powerful, there are still some things that he cannot do. For example, God cannot bring it about that he never existed, nor can he make a square that has less than four sides, nor can he make $1 + 1 = 890$. God cannot do things that are logically impossible because logically impossible tasks are not real tasks, they are pseudo-tasks. A logically contradictory state of affairs cannot exist. Even God cannot actualize a contradiction. This is not because he is limited in power—it is because a logically contradictory state of affairs doesn't actually describe anything. It is grammatical nonsense. One may as well say that God is limited in knowledge because he can't answer the

> **God cannot do things that are logically impossible because logically impossible tasks are not real tasks, they are pseudo-tasks.**

---

[3] A seminal work on this topic is Alvin Plantinga, *God, Freedom, and Evil* (Grand Rapids: Eerdmans, 1974).

question, "How many apples does a kilometre weigh?" To say that God cannot bring about the contents of grammatical nonsense—owing to the fact that *there is no content* in grammatical nonsense—hardly impugns his power and ability.

This point has been well understood in orthodox theology throughout the history of the church. It is true that some—eager to uphold the transcendence of God—have suggested that God can perform logically contradictory tasks. It has been impossible, however, to render their claims coherent (largely because coherence requires logic and the law of non-contradiction). Nobody can possibly explain what it means for God to be able to make the moon smaller than the earth and bigger than the earth at the same time and in the same way. It can't be explained because it is gibberish. Most believers who have given the matter serious consideration have concluded that God is all-powerful, but he cannot create the impossible (i.e. things that aren't actually things).

Libertarianism
The FWD combines this important principle with a particular view of freedom called *libertarianism*. Different philosophers have different views on the nature of freedom and responsibility, but libertarianism is the position that a free act cannot be determined by any factors whatsoever. In other words, if the performance of an act is inevitable, it cannot be done freely. For a person to be free, it must be within their power to either perform or refrain from performing the act. If their action is determined by factors outside their control, then it is not performed freely, and consequently they are not responsible for what they have done. For example, if a person is pushed over a cliff, they are not responsible for falling downward. The law of gravity determines what happens, entirely apart from their will. If all of our behaviour is the product of our genetics and environment—if everything we do is inevitable in scientific terms—then we are not free. Libertarians maintain that people have free will, and therefore at least some of what they think and do is not determined.

Theological determinism
Determinism can take many forms (genetic, sociological, scientific-materialistic, etc.), but the type of determinism that the FWD is mainly concerned with is theological determinism. *Theological deter-*

minism can take stronger or weaker forms, but the basic idea is that God can determine—either by direct ordination or by arranging circumstances—that human beings do what he wills them to do. If God acts this way, he may bring it about that humans do what he desires, but then they are not free in a libertarian sense. Theological determinism and libertarian free will are logically incompatible. This is highly significant. If God cannot do things that are logically incoherent, and theological determinism is logically incompatible with libertarian freedom, then God cannot create beings who have libertarian free will *and also* determine what these beings do.

God, freedom and control

If God has given human beings the gift of libertarian free will, he cannot determine how they will use it, since that would be a contradiction in terms. The very nature of libertarian freedom precludes such theological determinism. The FWD proposes that God not only decided to create beings with libertarian free will, he decided to create a universe where these creatures would have to make significant moral choices.

Alvin Plantinga (1932-) is the Christian philosopher whose work is widely regarded as having demonstrated that there is no logical contradiction between the existence of God and the existence of evil.

He did not create this world to be a luxury resort for human pampering. On the contrary, this world is full of opportunities to make choices that will have an incredible impact on ourselves and others—for either good or evil.

Part of God's intention for this world is that it is a place where human beings can learn how to responsibly care for one another. God's desire is that we use our freedom for the good of others, but he cannot determine that we do so. Libertarian freedom requires the opportunity and freedom to choose between good and evil. God cannot make us treat others well without violating our freedom, nor can he ensure that we will do what's right. We have the ability to love, protect and nurture, but we can also hate, kill and destroy. In libertarianism, the choice is up to us. Logically, God cannot determine our choice without violating the nature of our free will. This means that we alone are responsible for the moral evil that exists in the world.

As we have seen, the FWD recognizes that God cannot do things that are logically contradictory, and it is contradictory for God to ensure that people with libertarian free will always do what's right. Perhaps the biggest objection at this point is that the gift of libertarian free will is not worth the trouble it has caused. Two things are worth mentioning in response to this objection. The first is that this response does not address the *logical* problem of the existence of God and the existence of evil. In other words, our evaluation of whether this type of freedom was worth the evil it has generated is irrelevant to the question of whether or not the FWD solves the logical problem of the existence of God and the existence of evil. The second thing is that this evaluative judgement represents a personal, emotional opinion; it is not a logical argument. It is impossible to devise an objective formula that can be used to determine if the amount of evil in the world outweighs the value of the gift of freedom.

Advocates of libertarianism argue that without free will, people cannot be morally responsible for what they do. They insist that moral responsibility is a great good that is worth having, even if the mechanism that makes it possible (free will) is capable of being used to produce evil. Libertarians also tend to argue that free will is necessary for love. If we are determined to love someone, then we have no choice in the matter. How romantic is it to say that we love someone because the scientific laws of the universe necessitated that we would? The theological implications are that God cannot compel people to love him, since doing so contradicts the very essence of love. Neither can God compel people to love one another. God could have made people who were like preprogrammed robots, but he created free moral agents instead. In doing so, God gave them significant moral responsibility, which required libertarian free will, which by definition he cannot overrule without destroying, which would utterly defeat his original purposes! Therefore, concludes the FWD, God does indeed have a morally sufficient and good reason for allowing the existence of evil and suffering in the universe. Free will is exceptionally valuable and is necessary for the highest kinds of virtue, morality, responsibility and love. The existence of such things is greater than the existence of evil.

In relation to ethical systems, the FWD has a degree of flexibility. A non-consequentialist can argue that free will is intrinsically valuable, and therefore it is a good gift from God even if it is abused to generate evil. A consequentialist can argue that free will has produced a preponderance of good consequences over evil ones, so when all things are considered the world is better off with free will than without it. Even though there is moral evil that produces suffering, the good things that are made possible by free will—such as love, moral courage, genuine goodness, etc.—are worth it. The world contains evil, but on balance this world is more good than bad. There is love and harmony and beauty and goodness and moral responsibility. These are so valuable that they outweigh all the evil in the world. The FWD, therefore, is capable of evaluating free will as a worthwhile good on either a consequentialist or non-consequentialist ethical platform.

The free will defence, therefore, is capable of evaluating free will as a worthwhile good on either a consequentialist or non-consequentialist ethical platform.

At this point I must say that I am not particularly convinced that human beings actually have libertarian free will. That, however, is a topic for another day. I am not persuaded that libertarian free will is the *actual* explanation for why God has permitted the existence of evil: but the FWD does demonstrate that there is at least one *logically possible* way that the existence of God and the existence of evil are compatible. And since the FWD is designed to refute the claim that the existence of God and the existence of evil are logically contradictory, I believe that it successfully accomplishes its intended purpose.

2. The greater good defence

The second major defence is the *greater good defence* (GGD). This defence argues that God is justified in permitting the existence of evil if such evil is necessary for:

1. the production of a greater good, or,
2. the avoidance of a greater evil.

At first it might seem strange to suggest that one evil may be necessary to prevent the occurrence of a *greater* evil, but as anyone who has had a root canal understands, sometimes one pain is necessary to prevent greater pain down the road. As a result, it is entirely possible to justify bringing about pain (i.e. a dentist drilling) in order to avoid a greater pain (i.e. long term toothache, infection and bone decay). Amputating a gangrenous limb, as painful as both the short- and long-term effects will be, is permissible because it prevents an even greater loss in the future.

Inflicting a lesser pain to avoid a greater pain, however, assumes that at least some pain is unavoidable. But if God created the universe, why shouldn't it be pain free? One very common response to this question is that certain types of good are logically dependent on certain types of evil. These goods are referred to as "second-order goods." A first-order good is independent of evil. For example, love is inherently good. Love can exist even if evil doesn't. In contrast to love, consider a virtue like courage. It seems that courage can only exist where there is danger. We do not say that someone is courageous unless they are facing a situation that is dangerous or risky. Danger, however, by definition is a state where there is the potential for pain or loss. If there is no possibility for suffering, there is no danger, but if there is no danger, then there can be no courage, either.

> ...many people testify that it is through their trials that they have grown strong, clarified their priorities and values, and become more virtuous.

In a similar way, mercy, empathy and compassion are *responses* to suffering. Some of the heroes that we hold in the highest esteem are people who have made tremendous sacrifices and endured great personal hardships for the sake of others. We honour individuals who lay down their lives to save others—we say that they have made the supreme sacrifice—and they motivate us to put the needs of others ahead of our own. Such nobly heroic, self-sacrificial behaviour is only possible in a world where there is pain and suffering. Our greatest opportunities to exercise moral virtue often come when we are forced to face evil head-on.

Furthermore, many people testify that it is through their trials that they have grown strong, clarified their priorities and values, and become more virtuous. In fact, many people will claim that some of their most valuable experiences came through times of difficulty. If

God intended this world to be a place where people would have the opportunity to increase their virtues and grow morally stronger, then it is not surprising that this world would be full of adversity.

Remembering that the GGD only needs to show that it is logically *possible* for both God and evil to exist, the GGD must be judged successful. After all, it is entirely possible that the suffering and evil in the universe are necessary for the ultimate production of greater good in the end. Even if someone is skeptical that this will actually happen, it has to be acknowledged that it could *possibly* happen. And, to say it again, if it is possible then it is not logically contradictory.

EVIL AND EVIDENCE

As has been mentioned, academic philosophers—even those who are atheists—have acknowledged that there is no logical contradiction between the existence of God and the existence of evil. Nevertheless, some maintain that evil counts as evidence against the existence of God. They concede that it is *possible* for both God and evil to exist, but they believe it is *unlikely*. In broad terms, this is often referred to as *the evidential problem of evil*. Simply put, the existence of evil renders the existence of God improbable.

> *If it is possible for God to have a morally sufficient reason for permitting the existence of evil, how does evil count as evidence against his existence?*

To evaluate this claim, it is necessary to ask why evil counts as evidence against the existence of God. If it is possible for God to have a morally sufficient reason for permitting the existence of evil, how does evil count as evidence *against* his existence? In terms of epistemology, how could we know that evil is evidence against the existence of God, especially if we already know that God can have a good reason for allowing it to exist?

A little later on we will say more about how we assess evidence and probabilities, but for now we'll turn our attention to the two major arguments that come under the umbrella of the evidential challenge. The first challenge claims that there are some instances of evil that are pointless (these are referred to as *gratuitous* evils). The existence of these pointless evils is taken to be incompatible with the existence of God. The second challenge asserts that there is too much evil in the world (thus the issue concerns the *quantity* of evil). Both challenges recognize that the problem is not one of strict logical contradiction. Rather, the problem is with the perceived pointlessness of evil and the amount of evil in the world. These challenges are logically distinct, but in practice they are often combined. When they are conflated, the claim is usually that there is so much evil in the world some of it has to be pointless. Evil's gratuity is assumed on the basis of its volume.

1. The quantity of evil

In order to untangle the evidential argument, we will consider the issues of *gratuity* and *quantity* separately. This is necessary for more than one reason, but one such reason is that if the argument for the gratuitous nature of evil is dependent on the sheer *quantity* of evil in the world, then the atheist is making a dreadfully bad argument. The concept of quantity does not include the concept of gratuity. It is simply illogical to conclude that because there is a lot of something, some of it is pointless. Love is inherently good: the more love, the better. How strange to argue that because there is a lot of love in the world surely some of it is pointless! I have no idea how much food is required to feed the human population, but I assume it's a substantial quantity. If someone looked at the exact amount of food required to feed the world, and then declared: "That's an incredible tonnage of food. There's so much food here, surely some of it has to be pointless." We wouldn't likely be very impressed with their reasoning. Asking if there is a lot of something is one question; asking if something is pointless is another question altogether.

2. The gratuity or pointlessness of evil

The alleged *gratuity* of evil, rather than the *quantity* of evil, is where the challenge to theism really lies. The atheist claims that some evil in the world is gratuitous, and therefore it stands as evidence against the existence of God. At this point, the question that needs to be asked is, "How can we determine whether or not a particular instance of evil is gratuitous?" The atheist can assert that some evil is gratuitous, but supporting this claim is another matter.

It is important to remember that the evidential challenge is initiated by the atheist. The atheist is the one who claims that some evils are gratuitous. It is important to notice that the theist has not claimed that they know God's reason for allowing every particular example of evil that can be pointed out in the world. The theist is not claiming they know the reason behind every evil. The atheist is claiming they know *there is no reason*. Since the atheist is claiming that they know that some evil is gratuitous, the burden of proof falls on them to back up and justify their contention. The theist doesn't know why God has allowed *example of evil x*, but the atheist claims to know that *example of evil x* is pointless. But how can the atheist know that? There is really only one way: they must exhaustively comprehend the nature of reality and the entire course of history. In other words, they must know for sure that the evil was not tied to a greater good like the gift of free will, or that it will not produce greater goods in the future.

The limits of our knowledge
When the atheist claims that a particular example of evil is pointless, in practical terms, their claim amounts to the following: "I cannot see how there could be a point to this, therefore there is no point to this." Imagine a professor of mathematics (already a sad case, but about to get sadder), who puts a complex problem before her class, and is told by her first-year students that because they can't figure out the solution, there is no solution. Think of someone who is blind arguing that because they can't see any beauty in an art gallery, there is no beauty, and therefore art is useless. These analogies are clearly imperfect, but a better one—though still imperfect as all analogies are—is found by looking at the differences that exist between a parent and a child.

The terrorist attacks by the Islamic terrorist group al-Qaeda on the morning of September 11, 2001, awakened America to the inescapable reality of evil in the world. Evil is a feature of human experience that cannot be ignored or denied.

I have been blessed with two daughters who are still quite young, and, although this may sound trite, I love them very much. I never want them to be sad; I always want them to be happy. Yet, strangely, there are times when I find myself purposefully and intentionally making them unhappy. There are times when they want to eat too much sugar, and I say no. Conversely, there are times when they don't want to eat healthy snacks, but that's what they're given. Sometimes they want to spend too much time engaged with electronic entertainment. Sometimes they don't want to get fresh air and exercise outdoors. There are times they want to stay up well past their bedtime and don't like being told that they can't. Worse yet (from a child's perspective), there are times when their misbehaviour is met with disciplinary measures, none of which is ever pleasant at the time.

As they get older, they are becoming much more reasonable about such matters. They are beginning to see the relationship between actions and consequences. We have all witnessed toddlers having meltdowns because they have been told they can't have another cookie. Giving the benefit of the doubt to the parent who withheld the cookie, the question is, *could the parent actually have explained their reason to the child in a way that the child could accept?* Perhaps it's a nutritional concern. Well, the toddler doesn't share that particular concern. Perhaps they are told that a fifth cookie is not good for them. But, in the mind of the toddler, what could be worse than not getting the cookie?

Even more to the point, wise parents are trying to instill values and self-discipline in their children. They are trying, in age-appropriate ways, to get their children to realize that actions have consequences, that delayed gratification is necessary and good, that self-control is vital—all with the long-term goal of helping their children to grow up as healthy and helpful citizens. More crassly, they are trying to help their children avoid growing up into spoiled, demanding, self-centred, narcissistic adults (of which our society is not currently experiencing a shortage). A good parent, then, has certain long-term goals that are literally unimaginable to the toddler. No matter how carefully these goals are articulated, the toddler simply does not have the cognitive ability to grasp that the parent's decisions are governed by long-term goals that have the potential to produce profound goods.

Not only is it impossible for the toddler to understand the parent's time horizon, it is impossible for the toddler to understand the list of goods that the parent is working to see actualized. "Productive citizen" is a good that the parent identifies as worth pursuing. "Productive citizen" is a good that the toddler doesn't know exists and, furthermore, is incapable of understanding if informed.

The limitlessness of God's knowledge

To bring the discussion back to the issue of the gratuity of evil, we need to ask how persuasive we would find the toddler's case that, since they couldn't see why they were deprived of another cookie, there could be no possible reason behind their suffering. The argument amounts to: "I am eighteen months old and do not see what good can come from this. If I cannot see what good can come from this, then neither can my parents or anyone else. This means that no possible good can come from this. Therefore, my suffering is pointless." Now we will exchange the toddler for an atheist and replace the parent with God. The atheist's claim amounts to: "I am a human being, and I don't see what good can come from this. If I can't see what good can come from this, then neither could God. This means that no good can possibly come from this. Therefore, this is pointless." The atheist then takes the pointlessness of evil to constitute evidence against the existence of God.

> **The atheist's argument would be unassailable if there was reason to believe that their knowledge of every possible good was identical to God's.**

The atheist's argument would be unassailable if there was reason to believe that their knowledge of every possible good was identical to God's. If the atheist knew every imaginable good and every possible way to produce every good, then their analysis about the gratuitous nature of evil would be trustworthy. But why should anyone think that their index of goods is exhaustive? Why would we think that there are no goods except the ones that we can identify? We can rephrase the questions theistically: If God exists, would we expect that he doesn't know of any goods or morally valuable properties other than the ones that we know? If God exists, would we expect that he has no long-range goals other than ones *we* can imagine? If God exists, would we think that we would be in a position to know why he has allowed everything that we see? All we need to do is remember that God is omniscient, and then we will recognize that the difference between what he knows and what we know is *infinitely vaster* than the difference between what a toddler knows in comparison to their parent. Thus, there is absolutely no reason to think that, just because *we cannot see* the point behind a particular instance of evil, it must actually be pointless.

There is an implicit arrogance in thinking that everything an omniscient God knows about good and evil would be comprehensible to us. Wouldn't it seem likely that if God exists there would be many things he knows and does that would be utterly unfathomable and impenetrable to our finite minds? Let us mix our previous illustrations, and now place our toddler in the university mathematics course. Could any professor, no matter how gifted they were in communication, teach an eighteen-month-old child how to solve university-level math problems? If experience is any guide, the answer is obvious. But now imagine that God sat us down and explained his reasons for allowing all the evil and suffering that we see. Why would we think that we would be able to comprehend the answer? Isn't it possible that—just like the toddler in the university classroom—the subject matter is literally beyond our ability to grasp?

Atheism's logical problem

In terms of epistemology, then, the Christian has no reason to think that the atheist is in a position to know that any particular example of evil is actually pointless. But there is an even more devastating problem for the atheist's argument: it is logically circular. The defect is clear when the argument is cast in terms of questions and answers:

> Question 1: How do you know God doesn't exist?
> Answer 1:   Because of the existence of gratuitous evil.
> Question 2: How do you know that this evil is gratuitous?
> Answer 2:   Because God doesn't exist.

The atheist can only know that evil is gratuitous if they *already* know that God doesn't exist. However, the atheist's argument against the existence of God depends on *already* knowing that evil is gratuitous. In other words, the argument *already assumes* its conclusion. It simply begs the question. If an atheist can only know that evil is gratuitous because they already know that God doesn't exist, then they can't use the gratuity of evil as their *evidence* against God's existence in the first place. The argument fizzles out in a rational implosion.

As a matter of fact, a Christian can simply turn the tables and assert that if God exists then gratuitous evil doesn't—and since God does exist, therefore no evil is ultimately pointless. This isn't ducking the question. It only needs to be recalled that the Christian didn't claim they know why God has permitted every specific evil—it was the atheist who said they *know* that some evil is pointless. This means that the burden of proof lands on the shoulders of the atheist. After all, they're the one who insists that the gratuity of evil is evidence against the existence of God. The Christian has every reason to believe that an all-good and all-knowing God has many plans that go beyond their wisdom and comprehension. Since the atheist can't actually demonstrate their contention that a particular example of evil is genuinely gratuitous (besides the fact that they can't see a reason for it), the Christian has no reason to find this objection particularly compelling.

What is fair, however, is to wonder if there are any reasons why we should actually trust in God. Perhaps we can't know that evil is gratuitous, but why should we think that it isn't? In the end, I believe that Christians have every right and every reason to trust in God's goodness and wisdom, even in the face of incomprehensible evil and suffering. Going further, I think that *only* Christians have a worldview that provides a sufficient reason to trust in God in spite of the painful reality of evil. Philosophically, the existence of evil does not entail the conclusion that God does not exist. Theologically, however, the problem is actually capable of satisfactory resolution. It is not in contemporary philosophy, but rather in the pages of the Bible where we find the reason why we can trust God in the midst of a world full of evil and tragic suffering. In the following chapter we will see how this is so.

CHAPTER 5: SUMMARY AND APPLICATION

REMEMBER

> Even though I walk through the valley of the shadow of death, I will fear no evil, for you are with me; your rod and your staff, they comfort me (Psalm 23:4).

> And we know that in all things God works for the good of those who love him, who have been called according to his purpose (Romans 8:28).

REFLECT

1. How does the author respond to this apparent contradiction: "Isn't the presence of tragedy, sorrow and heartbreak incompatible with the existence of an all-good, all-powerful, all-knowing God? Doesn't this represent a great contradiction inside the Christian faith: a contradiction that disqualifies Christianity from being considered as a rational worldview?"

2. In the Christian worldview does *gratuitous* (pointless) *evil* exist?

3. Do you agree or disagree with the following statement: "Isn't it possible that—just like the toddler in the university classroom—the subject matter is literally beyond our ability to grasp?"

REJOICE

> God moves in a mysterious way
>   His wonders to perform;
> He plants His footsteps in the sea
>   And rides upon the storm.
>
> Deep in unfathomable mines
>   Of never failing skill

He treasures up His bright designs
    And works His sovereign will.

Ye fearful saints, fresh courage take;
    The clouds ye so much dread
Are big with mercy and shall break
    In blessings on your head.

Judge not the Lord by feeble sense,
    But trust Him for His grace;
Behind a frowning providence
    He hides a smiling face.

His purposes will ripen fast,
    Unfolding every hour;
The bud may have a bitter taste,
    But sweet will be the flower.

Blind unbelief is sure to err
    And scan His work in vain;
God is His own interpreter,
    And He will make it plain.

—William Cowper (1774)

William Cowper (1731-1800) was an accomplished poet, hymn writer and a friend of John Newton. Together they composed the *Olney Hymns* in the 1770s, of which this hymn is one of Cowper's most famous. Cowper suffered with severe depression throughout his life.

6

Christianity's great solution

In the previous chapter, we saw that proper philosophical analysis proves that the existence of God and the existence of evil are not logically contradictory. For those who have assumed that they are, this can be quite an important discovery. Others, however, continue to insist that evil counts as evidence against the existence of God. But this raises a very significant question: How do we assess and evaluate evidence in general? Even without always doing so self-consciously, we weigh evidence on the basis of things we already believe (our background knowledge). This truth still applies when we evaluate the evidence of evil.

For example, imagine that you were an eyewitness to many of the miracles that Jesus performed. Imagine further that you were a witness to the empty tomb and experienced his post-resurrection appearances. Given these circumstances, you would likely believe that Jesus was the Son of God. How could this belief be overturned? Would you end up rejecting your belief in Jesus because someone claimed that evil counted as evidence against the existence of God? Not likely. You would maintain your belief in Jesus despite the argument from evil, because you would evaluate it on the basis of your previous knowledge of Jesus' miracles and resurrection. You may not be able to explain *why* God permits evil, but the reality of evil would not convince you to reject the *reality* of the resurrection.

When we assess evidence and arguments, we do so on the basis of our worldview structures. The real issue for the Christian, then, is whether the biblical worldview can accommodate the existence of evil. We need to examine how evil fits into the Christian interpretation of reality. Our considerations of philosophy in the last chapter showed that the existence of both God and evil are logically consistent. Our first task in this chapter is to turn from philosophy to Scripture. The Christian worldview is founded on Scripture and shaped by Scripture, and it is in the pages of the Bible that we find the reason why we can trust in God despite the reality of evil, pain and suffering.

One of the first things that stands out about the Bible's treatment of evil is that it is not primarily philosophical. There are no abstract or theoretical treatments of the subject. Not a single author works out logical syllogisms. Not a single author weighs atheism against theism. The existence of God is axiomatic and assumed, and *that* is precisely what generates the tension. In the Scriptures, the problem of evil is a religious problem more than a philosophical problem. It produces the agonized cries of *Why?* and *How long?* rather than the speculative inquiries of armchair philosophers. The Bible is not primarily concerned with defusing atheism's objections. It is concerned with helping provide perspective to believers who are agonizing through their own personal experiences of suffering and evil.

There are several dimensions in the Christian perspective on evil that are embedded in a variety of biblical texts. Although there are passages in the Old Testament that deal with the subject of evil and suffering, the heart of the matter—and the biblical solution—is revealed in the New Testament. It is in the New Testament where we find the clearest revelation of God's plan for the world. It is through Jesus Christ that the purposes of God are fulfilled. This needs to be said because the Old Testament passages provide some helpful insight, but they do not provide a fully satisfactory answer. In the Old Testament, the existence of God is made plain, and his holiness is upheld, but exactly *why* he permits evil is left as a mystery. Like everything else in

Scripture, the key puzzle piece was missing until the coming of the Messiah. Until Jesus Christ lived, died and rose again, the picture couldn't make perfect sense. Even though God gave sufficient proof of his goodness in creation, and he continued to give people enough reason to trust him, the full proof of his love and goodness was only revealed in his Son the Lord Jesus Christ.

THE BOOK OF JOB

Before getting to Jesus, however, we will look at a biblical character who is practically synonymous with righteous suffering. The story of Job is unforgettable. Its plot plumbs the depth of human emotion and forces the reader to grapple with the stark reality of evil and the pain that it produces. Job experiences crushing emotional and physical agony, which plunge him into a spiritual crisis. The whole account cannot be reproduced here. What follows is a sketch: it will merely identify some of the major points that have a direct bearing on our topic—but only by reading Job itself can the artistry and poignancy be appreciated.

With God's permission, Job experienced crushing emotional and physical agony at the hand of Satan. Although God never revealed to Job what happened "behind the scenes," Job's faith in his God endured.

Like Charles Dickens' *A Christmas Carol*, the Book of Job begins with a statement that must be clearly understood, or nothing wonderful will be seen in the rest of the story. We are no sooner given Job's name than we are told that he: "was blameless and upright; he feared God and shunned evil" (Job 1:1). This is not only the narrator's view of Job. God *himself* declares in the heavenly court that: "There is no one on earth like [Job]; he is blameless and upright, a man who fears God and shuns evil" (1:8). Job is also characterized as "the greatest man among all the people of the East" (1:3).

If we had to pick someone whom God would *shield* from suffering and evil, it would be Job. But we are in for a surprise. Not only does God *not* prevent Job from suffering, God himself *points Job out* to Satan. God asks Satan if he has ever considered Job, and then extols Job's virtue (1:8). Satan replies that Job serves God because God has blessed him so abundantly. God knows this is false, so he grants Satan permission to test Job's righteousness and faith.

Satan gets to work, with the result that all of Job's fabulous wealth is lost. His servants are carried off by marauders. By far the worst thing that happens, however, is that Job's grown children are gathered at a feast, and the house where they are gathered collapses during a storm. Job's response, coming from the depths of incomprehensible pain, is to fall on the ground in mourning...and worship God. The Bible says that Job worshipped God, saying, "Naked I came from my mother's womb, and naked I will depart. The Lord gave and the Lord has taken away; may the name of the Lord be praised" (1:21). To this incredible response, the narrator adds the explanatory comment: "In all this, Job did not sin by charging God with wrongdoing" (1:22).

Notice three things from this first chapter of Job. First, *Job was absolutely righteous.* In fact, he was more blameless than anyone else around him. But righteousness is not a magic charm that keeps us from suffering in this world. As becomes apparent in the book, Job's friends were far less righteous and insightful than he was, but they did not suffer as he did. Any teaching that claims that God's followers can always expect to be healthy and wealthy in this world is a lie. Second, *God is in sovereign control over Satan, evil and suffering.* This is an extremely important point, and more will be said about it in due course. Third, *no matter what happens in our lives, it is wrong to charge God with wrongdoing.* In other words, there is never any justification for saying that God is guilty of a moral failure, or that he has somehow acted unrighteously. Job is in great anguish, but he worships. His pain is unfathomable, but he knows that God is not evil, and so he trusts that God has not done anything morally wrong.

In the next scene of the drama, God remarks to Satan that Job is still blameless and has held on to his integrity (2:3). Satan responds—with a complete misunderstanding of what motivates Job—that Job only worships God because his body has been left untouched. God tells Satan that Job's life must be spared, but Satan does as much as he can and inflicts Job's body with painful sores (2:7). Seeing her husband's misery, and speaking out of her own deep pain, Job's wife tells him to curse God and die. Job responds by asking the rhetorical question, "Shall we accept good from God, and not trouble?" (2:10).

Before going any further, there is something that we must imprint on our memories so that we can understand the plot of Job: *Job does not know about the conversations between God and Satan.* Crucially, only those who know what is happening in heaven can know what is really going on in Job's life. Everyone on earth—Job, his wife, his friends, his servants—is missing this key fact. As a result, it is impossible for them to fully understand what is happening. This is what Job knows: he has been blessed by God, he has prospered, he has not committed any egregious or flagrant sins and now he is suffering incalculable pain and loss in every area of his life. What he doesn't know is the answer to that most human of questions: *Why?*

Job's friends

As the book unfolds, Job is surrounded by a small group of friends who come to comfort and advise him. They give him their interpretations of the events, all of which are unhelpful, hurtful and completely wrong. The reader, of course, knows that Job's friends literally don't know what they're talking about—after all, they don't have access to the dialogue in the heavenly court—and their misdiagnoses are painfully inaccurate. Job's friends use a variety of arguments, but they all end up with basic variations of the following: God is good and Job is suffering, so Job must be being punished for doing something that was terribly wrong. It can hardly escape the notice of even the most inattentive reader that Job's friends are drawing a conclusion that is the complete opposite of the truth. Their analysis is 180 degrees off. God's verdict is that there is no one as blameless and righteous as Job. The verdict of Job's friends is that he cannot be blameless and righteous. In fact, they operate with a simplistic calculus where the greatness of Job's suffering is correlated and indexed to the greatness of his sin. Not surprisingly, they do not end up providing much comfort.

At no point does Job question whether God exists—he knows God exists. What he doesn't *know* is why God is permitting all this evil.

There are a lot of nuances in their individual speeches, and some twists and turns in the story, but the basic tension is that God, the reader and Job know that he is righteous, but his friends keep insisting that he isn't. In fact, according to their theology, he *can't* be righteous. Job dismisses their claims, simply because he knows that what they're saying about him is false.

But still, Job cannot figure out what God is doing. In fact, Job longs to have an audience with God where God will have to defend himself and explain his justice. At no point does Job question whether God exists—he knows God exists. What he *doesn't* know is why God is permitting all this evil.

Yet Job, just like his friends, at times seems to see justice, righteousness and suffering as parts of a mathematical equation. His friends look at his suffering, agree that God is just and then conclude that Job must be guilty of some great moral failure. Job looks at his suffering, knows that he is innocent of such a great moral failure and concludes that justice has miscarried. This is why Job desires an audience with God: he wants to know how justice and fairness and righteousness are being worked out in his life and *how God can defend himself*. Job will be the judge. He, not God, will be the one rendering the verdict.

Job meets God

Although this is what Job wants, he doesn't believe that he will get his day in court with God. He is wrong. God is going to meet with Job. Job's Creator grants his request for an audience. The encounter, however, unfolds very differently from the way Job envisioned. Job is not the one asking questions, nor is God required to plead his case. God—not Job—is the one who speaks and asks the questions. God—not Job—is the judge. It is only when Job accepts this arrangement that he ultimately finds satisfaction. In part, God vindicates himself to Job by showing that he doesn't need to vindicate himself to Job. Before Job can accept the righteousness of God's judgements, Job needs to realize that he isn't competent to stand in judgement on God in the first place. God guides Job to this realization, and, in doing so, God also gives Job the comfort that he needs.

God's opening statement begins a line of reasoning that is exactly what Job needs. God begins by asking, "Who is this that obscures my plans with words without knowledge? Brace yourself like a man; I will question you, and you shall answer me" (Job 38:2–3). Even though God has drawn close to Job, God is still high above him. Job has been speaking without knowledge. He has not been able to understand what has been happening, yet, as time has gone on, he has begun to think that God is treating him unfairly and denying him justice. This is a crucial point that must be borne in mind throughout God's speech: Job has been speaking "words without knowledge." God will address the relationship between evil, justice and his rule over the universe, but the initial point concerns *epistemology*. Job—and by extension his friends—simply lack the necessary knowledge that is required to comprehend and judge God's moral governance of the universe.

After this opening statement, God begins to question Job. This is the opposite of the way that Job had envisioned his day in court with God. Unfortunately, God's line of questioning has often been misinterpreted. God asks Job multiple questions about the physical world—questions that Job cannot answer. Job is forced to acknowledge that he doesn't understand how the world was formed, nor does he understand how the world continues to function. He isn't the one who created the earth, designed the oceans or suspended the stars in space. Job doesn't make it rain or orchestrate the majesty of a thunderstorm. Of course, Job knows *some* things about the world, but his understanding is extremely limited. Like every single one of us, Job knows only an infinitesimal fraction of all there is to know.

God's speech to Job is not an exercise in missing the point, as some atheists have asserted. God does not answer Job's deep pain and emotional experience of morality, evil and justice by saying things that are irrelevant. God's response is not, "Job, you're struggling with my justice, but don't forget I can make an ostrich." Everything God says is tailored precisely to the struggle Job is having. God is building a logical case that, in the end, will be a great help to Job. God begins by talking about the physical world, but this is only the first part of his speech. At this point, God is establishing an epistemological and theological framework in which Job will be able rest and find comfort.

Even though Job has been powerfully reminded of his very limited knowledge, the reader knows that Job doesn't even know all that he doesn't know. His knowledge of the visible, earthly realm is paltry. His knowledge of the invisible, heavenly realm is nil. If Job knows very little about the world he sees, he knows nothing of the world he can't see. Since the universe consists of both the visible and invisible realms—and since the latter is far more significant than the former—

Our perspective is too finite and our knowledge is far too limited for us to imagine that we are qualified to stand in judgement on God.

nobody on earth is in a position to evaluate the workings of God in the created universe. Our perspective is too finite and our knowledge is far too limited for us to imagine that we are qualified to stand in judgement on God.

Having humbled Job (not humiliated him), God gives Job permission to bring his charges against him, and to argue his case (40:1–2). Job, however, acknowledges that there is nothing he can say against God (40:3–5). God has helped Job see that Job does not—indeed, cannot—know better than his Maker. As a result, Job has accepted that he does not know enough to accuse God of wrongdoing. This point is foundational for God's next line of discourse. God begins by asking Job the rhetorical questions: "Would you discredit my justice? Would you condemn me to justify yourself?" (40:8). Atheistic caricatures aside, God is perfectly aware that his ability to create stars and eagles does not provide a satisfactory solution to the problem of evil. The relevant principle is not sheer creative power, but wisdom and control. Humans have extraordinarily limited knowledge, and even less wisdom. How can they stand in judgement on the wisdom of God? Why would they think they can condemn God's justice? Barely able to manage their own lives (at best), why would people think they know how God should manage the entire *universe*?

God's ability to create stars and eagles sets the groundwork for explaining the principle of wisdom and control to Job—Job's understanding is *finite*, God's is *infinite*.

The point should be granted that human beings are too limited to pass judgement on God. Anyone who spends time reflecting on how little they know about the physical world and animal kingdom should recognize the profound limitations of their knowledge. But God moves from this relatively obvious principle to a more significant one. Job's understanding is *finite*, but God's is *infinite*. The world that Job barely understands is a world not only fully *comprehended* by God; it is *created* and *controlled* by God. There is nothing in the physical universe that exists independently from God.

But is God also in full control of the spirit world? After all, Job's problems in the physical realm are generated by events in the spiritual world (a world of which Job remains in complete ignorance). The real question is whether God is the master of *everything* on earth and in heaven. The answer to this question is a resounding, "Yes!" But the way God describes his control of heaven and the spirit realm can easily be misunderstood by people who are not familiar with Job's cultural milieu. In order to comprehend the point of God's second discourse, the reader needs to understand what God means when he refers to "Leviathan."[1]

In Job's day, Leviathan was the name of a Canaanite deity. Leviathan was evil, he was very strong, and he stirred up trouble and chaos. He lived in the sea and could not be mastered or domesticated by human beings. In God's second discourse, he declares that he is the master of everything, including Leviathan. No finite human being can set limits on Leviathan, but God can. As a demonic god, Leviathan is a perfect symbol for the serpent, Satan. Job is well aware that the Leviathan figure cannot be matched or defeated by human knowledge or power. As a result, human beings live in a world that is also the abode of a powerful being who is characterized by darkness, chaos and malevolence. No one on earth can see, understand or control him. The real Leviathan, in biblical terminology, is Satan—the same powerful, evil being that we met in the very first chapter of Job—the being who is responsible for afflicting Job with pain and suffering, and the one who is bent on harm and destruction. Even Leviathan/Satan is under the authority of God. He is not the evil equal of God. He is a controlled creature.

Job's limited knowledge of the physical world is again contrasted with God's perfect knowledge and control of the physical world. Likewise, Job's virtually non-existent knowledge of the spirit world is contrasted with the fact that God fully knows and controls it. As a result, Job is in no position to discredit God's justice. God is continually at work in the universe to bring about justice in a way that goes beyond human comprehension. As Job ponders these things, he concludes that, "Surely I spoke of things I did not understand, things too wonderful for me to know" (42:3b). Our infinitesimal knowledge, understanding and wisdom should drive us to the same conclusion: When we start to discredit the justice of God, we don't know what we are talking about.

---

[1] See Job 41. An excellent treatment of the nature of Leviathan is found in Robert S. Fyall, *Now My Eyes Have Seen You: Images of Creation and Evil in the Book of Job*. New Studies in Biblical Theology (Downers Grove: IVP, 2002).

God himself is the answer

At this juncture, the conclusion is only one of negation (i.e. we don't know enough to discredit God's justice), but the ultimate conclusion to the Book of Job is positive. In the end, Job's heart is not satisfied with the simple recognition that he is too limited to judge God. Job is only satisfied when he beholds the majestic purity of the transcendent Creator. When Job sees God, his questions melt away—not because God has told him the answer, but because God *himself* is the answer. God's holy presence is beyond reproach. Job is forced to exclaim, "My ears had heard of you but now my eyes have seen you" (42:5). Doubts about God's character and purposes cannot be maintained in the light of his glory. As children derive comfort from hugs rather than explanations, so Job finds comfort in the *presence* of God. Propositional truth and objective facts—when interpreted by someone with extraordinarily limited knowledge—can only go so far. The limits of human thought are transcended by the living God, not because his being is irrational, but because he is *suprarational*. He is not less than what human beings can comprehend—he is infinitely more. In the presence of God, all Job's queries are swallowed up into an unfathomable, bottomless ocean of infinite goodness, wisdom and power. Job is humbled. God is exalted. Job is satisfied *not because God has answered his questions* but because Job has *seen the God who has the answers*. Moreover, he has seen the God who *is* the answer.

God's good purposes

The Book of Job ends with God blessing Job with an abundance that surpassed what he had before he experienced the attack of the Leviathanic Satan. Some people have argued that this ending is anticlimactic and out of step with real life. In real life, they argue, people often suffer losses that are never restored. The point, however, is not that God will ensure that people who suffer in this world are always satisfactorily compensated in the here and now. The real point is that despite sin, pain, disease, death, suffering, anguish, evil, chaos and the Devil himself, in the end God is in control, working all things out in this world in a way that is right and beautiful, proper and good. God is even able to work through the evil acts of wicked people (and demonic powers) to bring about ultimate good. People are able to exercise their wills for good or for evil, but God has the divine ability to bring good out of the evil things they do. Real evil exists in the universe, but it is not out of control. Evil cannot defeat God's good purposes. It exists, but God conquers it by bringing good out of it. How God ultimately does this is found at the centre of the biblical storyline.

CHRIST AND EVIL

The Book of Job introduces us to this truth, but the climactic revelation awaits Jesus Christ. In previous chapters, we noted that the cross is central in Christian theology. Every passage in the Bible leads toward the cross or flows out of it. Every key point of theology is related to, and interpreted by, the cross of Christ. Without overstatement, we can confidently say that *the cross of Jesus Christ is the main event in the history of the world*. It was planned in the counsel of God's wisdom before the first act of creation. This whole created order was designed as a theatre for the glory of God, and God's glory is most fully displayed in the passion of Jesus Christ, the one and only Son of God.

The cross of Christ lies at the centre of human history. Here, infinite love met with pure hatred. In an amazing paradox, what was meant for incredible evil was simultaneously used for the best possible good—reconciliation with God.

From one perspective, there has never been anything more pleasing, good, noble, holy, loving or supremely valuable as the cross of Christ. Viewed from another perspective, there has just as truly never been a more wicked, malicious, unjust, evil, dark and morally horrific event as the crucifixion of Christ. It was there that the only morally perfect person in the history of the world was betrayed, degraded, tortured and ruthlessly murdered in the most agonizing way possible. Infinite love was met with pure hatred. Jesus, the one who loved, taught, blessed, healed and liberated, was killed in cold blood by the very people he came to help.

Homicide is always terrible. matricide, the killing of one's mother, is worse. Regicide, the killing of a king or ruler, is normally punished more strictly than regular homicide, because of the chaos it can produce in society. At the cross, the worst type of murder imaginable was attempted—the crowd tried to commit deicide: they tried to kill God. Jesus was God the Son incarnate. He was a perfect man but remained the perfect God. Those who crucified Jesus, murdered the only perfect man who ever lived, and they also attempted to kill God himself, all in the same act. From this angle, the wickedest thing people have ever done was done at the cross of Christ.

The paradox of the cross

This raises a very interesting question: *How can the same event be simultaneously the best and worst event in the history of the world?* As we have seen, it is partly a matter of perspective. At the cross, God secures salvation for sinners. At the same cross, sinners murder the only perfect person in history, and they attempt to murder God. The people who acted were trying to bring about something *unspeakably evil*. The God who acted was bringing about *incalculable good*. Acts 2:23 says, "This man [Jesus] was handed over to you by God's deliberate plan and foreknowledge; and you, with the help of wicked men, put him to death by nailing him to the cross." Notice that the people who acted to crucify Jesus are described as *wicked*, but nevertheless they still bring about the good that God intended. God does not force them to crucify his Son against their will. He is in control, but does not coerce. Even the cross of Christ—brought about by wicked men—is part of the plan of God that results in the best ends.

Through the cross of Christ, sin and guilt are dealt with. God and human beings are reconciled. By the wonder of the cross, people can move from death to life. They can be restored to what they were meant to be. Furthermore—having justly dealt with sin—God is not only saving people from eternal punishment, he is preparing to recreate the universe into a new heaven and new earth, the home of righteousness. Make no mistake, there was no possible way for there to be a happy and holy home for human beings apart from Christ's sacrificial death in their place. On a consequentialist understanding of ethics, therefore, God's work at the cross is the most morally perfect reality in the history of the universe.

On a non-consequentialist understanding of ethics, the cross is intrinsically the supreme exemplification of all that is morally right and good. It was there that the Son of God incarnate humbly and willingly submitted to death so that he could save the very race of rebels who, blinded by their hatred, wanted to rid the universe of him once and for all. Sinners are rebels because Jesus is their lawful king. But more than this, he is their Maker, Creator and Sustainer. And he loves them. He loves them infinitely and perfectly. His perfect love is repaid with hate. His offer of love and life is met with rejection and death. There has never been a greater love nor a more noble, and—literally—self-sacrificial act. There has never been a group of people who deserved less but were given more. Christ on the cross is the supreme good. Christ on the cross secures the greatest ends. As set forth in the plan of God, therefore, the cross is the highest good in either consequentialist or non-consequentialist terms. Considered on the basis of its intrinsic nature, it is morally flawless. Evaluated on the basis of its consequences, it is unsurpassable.

> **If God can bring the greatest good out of the worst that evil beings can do, then we can trust that there is never an evil out of which God cannot bring greater good.**

None of this overturns the fact that *people have never acted with more wicked intentions than they did at the cross*. This, however, is what allows us to trust God *no matter what takes place*. God shows us through Job that we are not in a position to comprehend the universe, and as a result we are not in a position to judge his justice. Yet, in the Book of Job, we also saw that God controls the universe, including Satan and the forces of chaos and evil. But, it is at the cross that we see proof that God can indeed control Satan and evil people who are doing their worst. Evil was darkest at the cross—but through the evil acts of evil agents, God secured the greatest good imaginable. The conclusion we are justified in drawing is this: *If God can bring the greatest good out of the worst that evil beings can do, then we can trust that there is never an evil out of which God cannot bring greater good.* Since this is true, Christians have every right to believe that the existence of evil does not create an overwhelming difficulty for the Christian faith. In fact, the cross of Jesus Christ is conclusive proof—logical, as well as historical—that evil does not count as evidence against the Christian worldview.

This does not mean that we will ever know exactly *why* individual events happen. I don't know why certain disasters strike, why particular people suffer in particular ways, why *event x* happened to *person y* (and not to *person z*), etc. Frankly, I doubt I could understand the entire master plan of God in all of its details, even if it was explained to me. But what I do know is that the wickedest act generated by the wickedest intentions of the wickedest people was used by God to redeem and save a fallen world. If God can do *that*, there is nothing he cannot do.

It is this reality that allows believers to trust in God's promises. One of the most precious verses to many Christians is Romans 8:28: "And we know that in all things God works for the good of those who love him, who have been called according to his purpose." How can we have confidence that God is working in all things for our good? Or, perhaps more to the point, how can we know that God is *successfully* working in all things for our good? The answer, of course, is the cross. If God can work the cross out for our good, then there is nothing that is too evil to be redeemed by his wisdom and power.

This is why Paul can say, "We are more than conquerors through him who loved us" (Romans 8:37). Someone who conquers an enemy is victorious, but they may be terribly injured in the fight. Their enemy may not prevail, but they may still inflict a great deal of harm before they are defeated. A conqueror, then, may suffer great loss in their victory. To be more than a conqueror means, however, that our enemies not only fail to *hurt* us, they actually *help* us! The same God who brought good out of the evil at the cross can bring blessing and good to us—not merely in spite of the wicked acts of our enemies, but *through* them. In the plan of God, the enemies of his children only succeed in being a source of blessing to them in the end. Christians not only conquer, they *more* than conquer.

JOSEPH AND EVIL

We see this principle at work in Genesis, the first book of the Bible. In a very familiar narrative, Joseph's brothers sell him to slave traders in a passing caravan, and he ends up as a slave in Egypt. Through the plan of God, Joseph is eventually exalted to a high position in the land. God reveals to Joseph that there is going to be a severe famine for seven years, and Joseph is able to put a plan in place that saves Egypt and her neighbours from complete devastation. Due to the famine, Joseph's brothers are forced to come to Egypt to get grain, and they are brought into Joseph's presence. In a scene full of drama and emotion, Joseph reveals his identity to his brothers. Genesis 45:4–8 records the event:

> Then Joseph said to his brothers, "Come close to me." When they had done so, he said, "I am your brother Joseph, the one you sold

into Egypt! And now, do not be distressed and do not be angry with yourselves for selling me here, because it was to save lives that God sent me ahead of you. For two years now there has been famine in the land, and for the next five years there will be no plowing and reaping. But God sent me ahead of you to preserve for you a remnant on earth and to save your lives by a great deliverance.

"So then, it was not you who sent me here, but God. He made me father to Pharaoh, lord of his entire household and ruler of all Egypt."

Notice that Joseph says—more than once—that *his brothers* sold him into slavery. Notice further that Joseph also says—more than once—that *God* sent him to Egypt. In fact, Joseph's conclusion is: "it was not you who sent me here, but God." Yet his brothers *did* sell him into slavery. Nothing excuses them, nothing makes their part of things acceptable, and nothing that God did through their actions lessens their responsibility. God, however, was able to work through their evil to bring about great good. In a way that can't help but remind us of the cross of Christ, the evil act and intentions of Joseph's brothers were used by God to accomplish the great good of saving many lives. Ironically, in the providence of God, some of the lives that were saved belonged to the individuals who had sold Joseph into slavery. They had tried to get rid of Joseph, but God used him to save their lives.

At the end of Genesis, Joseph and his brothers experience the death of their father. Now, Joseph's brothers worry that Joseph will get revenge on them. But Joseph reassured them, saying, "You intended to harm me, but God intended it for good to accomplish what is now being done, the saving of many lives" (Genesis 50:20). In Joseph's slavery—as in Christ's cross—evil people act with evil intentions, but a righteous God acts in the same event and succeeds in bringing about the great good of saving many lives. God was at work for Joseph's good even when his enemies sold him into slavery. God not only ensured that Joseph conquered his enemies, he made sure that Joseph was *more* than a conqueror. The very thing they thought would destroy him was used by God for his good and the good of countless others.

This does not mean that Joseph knew everything that the future held when he was first sold into slavery. It doesn't mean that the disciples knew, when Jesus was dying on the cross, that immeasurable blessing would flow from his death—blessing that would transform the entire universe and save many lives. It certainly doesn't mean that all suffering is a sham or a fake, or that if you have strong faith you'll be immune to grief. Faith and tears are not incompatible. Furthermore, this doesn't mean that we will always *perceive* the good that God is bringing out of the evil we experience (the good may come to flower in the next generation, or it may await the new heavens and earth, or it just may be too subtle for our spiritual senses to detect). Nevertheless, God has given us more than enough examples of his ability to bring good out of evil for us to be able to trust him. Our faith in him is not blind. It is a rational response to his proven abilities.

Faith and tears are not incompatible.

A CRUCIFORM WORLDVIEW

It is time to bring the observations of this chapter together, and then briefly look at one more passage of Scripture. First, we see in Job that our knowledge is so limited that we are not able to stand in judgement on the justice of God. He is in control of the physical and spiritual realms, and he is able to make all things right in the end. Second, we see that God is more than able to work all things together for good. This includes all the events that were brought about by the malevolence of Leviathan, the jealousy of Joseph's brothers and the world's hatred for Christ. No matter what the forces of evil try to do to believers, God's children are more than conquerors. Third, it is only at the cross that the tension between the existence of God and the existence of evil is satisfactorily resolved. Not only does the Christian worldview account for both the existence of God and the existence of evil, it is the only worldview that can do so. No other religion can reconcile the reality of evil and the reality of the goodness of God. This is because it is the only worldview that is based on the cross. It is the only worldview that is cruciform.

A peace that transcends understanding

Our hope is not in facts and propositional truths—it is in a personal being of perfect love and power. This is why it is a profound mistake to attempt to reason about the existence of God and the existence of evil apart from recognizing the personal and relational dynamic that exists between God and his children. Job was satisfied when he *met* God. Christians are satisfied when they meet God through Jesus Christ. This personal relationship is stronger than any abstract argumentation. (Although, for what it's worth, we have seen that there is no logical argument that refutes the Christian worldview on the basis of the existence of evil.)

It also means that God can provide his children with resources that simply cannot be accounted for on the basis of an atheist's worldview. God is perfectly capable of drawing his children close to him and comforting them in his way and in his time. In the apostle Paul's letter to the Philippians, Paul writes, "And the peace of God, which transcends all understanding, will guard your hearts and minds in Christ Jesus" (Philippians 4:7). When we are walking with God and praying to him (see Philippians 4:6), God can give us a peace that we cannot understand, let alone explain to others.

I have personally known numerous Christians who have gone through the worst kinds of tragedies and experienced the most poignant losses, and yet they are still rejoicing in the Lord. Many times I have been struck by the fact that *I just can't understand* how people can walk through their darkest valleys. But I shouldn't be able to understand, because God can give his children a peace that *transcends all understanding*. It is literally supernatural and personal, and as such it cannot be understood nor explained by the natural and impersonal worldview of materialism.

> **...the living God of the Christian faith is able to personally strengthen and comfort his people in a way that provides emotional and existential rest.**

In comparison to the experienced peace of God, the worldview challenges of evil fade into insignificance. This relationship that exists between God and his child—won through the cross—provides a comfort that quells fears and subsides doubts. The Christian worldview is not only philosophically equipped to handle the problem of evil, the living God of the Christian faith is able to personally strengthen and comfort his people in a way that provides emotional and existential rest. We are more than conquerors through the cross of Christ and the personal presence of the living and loving God. And there is no good reason to think otherwise.

CHAPTER 6: SUMMARY AND APPLICATION

REMEMBER

I know that my redeemer lives, and that in the end he will stand on the earth (Job 19:25).

You intended to harm me, but God intended it for good to accomplish what is now being done, the saving of many lives (Genesis 50:20).

Fellow Israelites, listen to this: Jesus of Nazareth was a man accredited by God to you by miracles, wonders and signs, which God did among you through him, as you yourselves know. This man was handed over to you by God's deliberate plan and foreknowledge; and you, with the help of wicked men, put him to death by nailing him to the cross. But God raised him from the dead, freeing him from the agony of death, because it was impossible for death to keep its hold on him (Acts 2:22–24).

REFLECT

1. Joseph's brothers expected payback, but Joseph saw that God used evil for good (Genesis 50:20). How does this truth apply to your life? How would you counsel other Christians going through adversity?

2. Regarding the cross, how can the same event simultaneously be the best *and* worst event in the history of the world? Please explain and illustrate in your own words.

3. The Christian worldview accounts for the existence of God and evil. How does this communicate peace to others?

REJOICE

Great Captain of salvation,
   Now crowned with highest glory,
     Joyful we raise,
     Our songs of praise,
   And lowly bow before Thee:
We worship and adore Thee,
   Each heart and tongue confessing,
     Worthy to reign,
     The Lamb once slain,
   Of honour, power and blessing.

Thou hast the cross endurèd—
   In love beyond all measure!
     The curse, the grave,
     Thy saints to save,
   And have us as Thy treasure.
We see Thee as the Victim,
   Our sins and sorrows bearing;
     The Lamb once slain,
     Alive again,
   The crown of glory wearing.

Head of the new creation,
   To God's right hand ascended;
     Thy saints rejoice,
     With heart and voice,
   Before Thy feet low bended:
We own Thee, Lord, exulting
   In all Thy joy and glory:
     And long to be
     On high with Thee,
   Where all shall bow before Thee.

—James George Deck (1837)

Interlude

In the first part of this book, we considered some of the major points involved in worldview analysis. Although much more could be said, and many more issues discussed, we also examined some of the critical issues that concern the rationality of the Christian faith. Much of the discussion was relatively abstract—it was geared for the intellect. In other words, the first part was about *knowing*—this second part is more about *caring*. Only when our knowledge is matched by our care, will people care about our knowledge. God's plan for defending our faith involves our head, our heart and our hands.

The popular adage, "People won't care how much you know until they know how much you care," is not an ironclad rule, but it does make a fair point. Of course, people *do* care about what we know, especially when we are talking with them about issues of ultimate importance, like the existence of God and the truth of Jesus Christ. It is necessary to be able to explain the basics of our faith and articulate the gospel. It is also necessary, however, that we do so in the proper spirit. Christians should demonstrate genuine care and concern for everyone. Knowledge and virtue are mutually reinforcing. On the one hand, when you care about people, they tend to be more receptive to what you say, and, on the other hand, when you spend time engaging in positive dialogue, people find out that you really care about them.

Care and concern are never merely theoretical. They always manifest themselves in practical ways. The Book of James contains a stinging critique of religious hypocrisy. James writes:

> What good is it, my brothers and sisters, if someone claims to have faith but has no deeds? Can such faith save them? Suppose a brother or a sister is without clothes and daily food. If one of you says to them, "Go in peace; keep warm and well fed," but does nothing about their physical needs, what good is it? In the same way, faith by itself, if it is not accompanied by action, is dead. But someone will say, "You have faith; I have deeds." Show me your faith without deeds, and I will show you my faith by my deeds (James 2:14–18).

The absence of deeds is indicative of the absence of faith, and the example James provides involves the incredibly practical matter of helping the poor. If a poor person comes looking for material assistance, and they are met with nothing but religious platitudes, the only truth that has been revealed is the truth that the religious individual is a hypocrite. Where there is truth and faith, there is love and good deeds.

The following chapters investigate emotions, morality, beauty, virtue and charity. Although there are some intellectual arguments, the shift is away from abstraction and theory to concrete duty and practice. Proclaiming and defending the faith takes place with our entire lives, both in every word we speak and everything we do. The Christian faith is not merely a private affair, a transaction between God and the individual that only affects their soul. Christianity transforms lives, and results in love for others. This love motivates practical service, acts of compassion, deeds of mercy and sacrifice. At its best, the church in history has served humanity, fed the poor, cared for orphans and widows (i.e. the most vulnerable and marginalized) and fought for social justice. Christians are called to think, speak and act in light of Christ's light. We are called to love as God has loved us.

There is more theory in the following pages, but the theory flows into practical application. If the first part of this book was focused on the *head*, this second part is focused on our *hearts* and our *hands*. Christians individually, and the church collectively, are to show the world how the gospel of Jesus Christ has transformed their lives. When the rationality of the faith is placed in the context of a life of love and service, this holistic witness is powerful and persuasive.

We will now begin to think about how the Christian faith makes sense of ethics, values and beauty (i.e. aesthetics), and how it motivates us to live in a way which is pleasing and honouring to God, as well as vitally helpful for all people, at all times and in all places.

7

Values, beauty and fulfillment

As we briefly sketched a Christian response to the problem of evil in the previous two chapters, we were working with one massive assumption: *We were assuming that evil is evil.* We were also assuming that there are rational grounds for differentiating between right and wrong, good and evil, justice and injustice, morality and immorality. We simply accepted that these concepts are intelligible. Whenever someone cites the existence of evil as a reason for disbelieving in the existence of God, they are operating on the principle that there is a right way for God to act. There are things that God should do, and things that he should not do. Our views concerning what God ought and ought not to do are based on our prior understanding (even if vague) of the nature of goodness and morality.

If we are being honest, we know that our moral judgements are at least as emotional as they are rational. Some people go so far as to argue that our ethical views are literally nothing more than the product of our feelings. They maintain that, in just the same way as we find rotten food disgusting, we find certain behaviours disgusting. These feelings of revulsion are subsequently rationalized and placed in a mental compartment we label *morality*. In this interpretation of morality, the following three statements really amount to the same thing:

1. I believe that murder is immoral.
2. I find murder disgusting.
3. I don't like murder.

It is important to notice that this approach to morality can tell you something about someone's *feelings* about various things, but nothing about the *nature* of the things themselves. I may not like broccoli, but that doesn't show that it has the intrinsic property of being disgusting. I may not like murder, but what does that prove? It does not take a keenly trained logical eye to see that the claims, "I don't like murder," and "Murder is evil and immoral," are hardly identical, nor is there a necessary, logical bridge from the former to the latter.

Nevertheless, there is an intuition underlying this interpretation of morality that is extremely important. Emotions play an enormous role in our ethical evaluations. But so should our intellects. Moral judgements are too important to be left to the whim of our feelings. We simply can't, however, suppress our emotional responses to moral realities. How we feel about them is a necessary part of reaching proper moral conclusions. We are not calculators. We cannot determine right and wrong using algorithms and abstract reasoning alone.

When we begin to take this matrix of emotional and intellectual interaction seriously, we discover a chicken-or-the-egg type dilemma. Aristotle recognized that a person needed to be virtuous in order to form accurate moral judgements. He believed that when a virtuous person discerns the most virtuous pathway, they take it. This exercise in virtue confirms their virtuousness and strengthens it. Thus, a virtuous person grows in virtue throughout the course of their lifetime. In this process, virtue is required for virtue, virtue leads to virtue and virtue is necessary in order to recognize the virtuous course of action. But where do you start if you aren't very virtuous in the first place? (The same type of problem is discussed in the world's great wisdom literature: It takes wisdom to discern wise teaching, and wisdom to practice it. A wise person will grow in wisdom, but how can a fool begin to become wise?)

We will not try to solve this dilemma here. (Hint: the Christian response has a prominent place for grace and God's intervening help.) For now, it is sufficient to observe that *our views on morality are generated at the intersection of our intellectual and emotional faculties*. One of the huge advantages of the Christian worldview is that it takes this intellectual-emotional reality of our human experience seriously. Christianity has a significant place for value and values. Morality, ethics and virtue are all at home in the Christian worldview. They are not considered in a cold, calculating, abstract or dispassionate fashion. On the contrary, in Christian theology, moral values are vibrant and lively. They are infused with colour and beauty. In fact, beauty itself—and our aesthetic experience of it in art, music, dance, literature, etc.—thrives in Christianity. This is worthy of reflection and meditation.

We have spent time considering the fact that the world contains a great deal of suffering and evil. The counterbalancing truth is that the world is also full of beauty, goodness, value and joy. There is evil, but there is good. In fact, the existence of evil is parasitic on goodness. Evil is a negation. Its existence consists in the entirely negative sphere of deforming and devaluing, the same way that sickness can only exist as a negation of health. All of this assumes that proper forms and values pre-exist their deformations: parasites require hosts. To judge something as evil is to say that it ought not to be, something has gone wrong, something inherently positive has been compromised. Identifying something as evil rests on the tacit assumption that *there is good*—and the good is something logically prior and deeper. It is foundational and an integral part of the fabric of reality.

Those who endorse ethical relativism don't live out their view for more than a minute.

MORALITY AND MATERIALISM

All worldviews must accommodate the fact that morality is a deeply integrated and foundational part of reality. It is no good to say that morality and its negation in evil are illusory or unreal. Human beings are inescapably moral beings. Ethical relativists are a dime a dozen in the classroom, but nowhere to be found in the real world. Those who endorse ethical relativism don't live out their view for more than a minute. Reality has a way of popping pretentions. People may deny the objectivity of morality, but they can never do so with consistency—either in theory or in practice. We have no choice but to take moral standards and axioms as givens (given by God, declares the Scriptures). A potentially acceptable worldview, therefore, must be able to coherently relate objective moral standards to the metaphysical structure of the universe. Attempting to provide an intelligible account of the relationship between morality and metaphysics is one of the weakest points of naturalistic worldviews.

First, it must be noted that many naturalists recognize that objective morality is incoherent given the assumptions of a materialistic worldview. Materialists posit a universe that came into existence from an absolute nothingness without any governing rationality behind it or purpose for it. With these origins it is virtually impossible to avoid the conclusion that the universe is not originally moral, nor is morality found within it. Nothingness is completely void of moral properties. Did the moral properties pop into existence out of nothing when the singularity appeared, or were they produced by the force of the Big Bang? Many atheist philosophers have rejected the idea of objective morality and ethics, simply because such things do not fit coherently into their understanding of the nature of the universe. Secular humanists who attempt to hold to both objective morality and materialist atheism are swamped in contradictions, regardless of how self-assured their claims.

> **Many atheist philosophers have rejected the idea of objective morality and ethics, simply because such things do not fit coherently into their understanding of the nature of the universe.**

For the sake of the narrative, we will grant that the impossible happened and the universe came into existence out of nothing. Even if this is how the physical universe began, we have discovered nothing about the *origins* of morality. The universe certainly wasn't a moral system during the first minute of its existence. In fact, the materialist maintains that throughout billions of years matter moved through the universe, colliding, uniting, dividing, building and destroying. Even today, we see matter in motion, where one material entity collides with another and causes great damage. A meteor collides with a moon, or a supernova destroys neighbouring planets. The resulting destruction is catastrophic, yet it would be entirely inappropriate to say that the destruction should be interpreted in moral categories. An asteroid may destroy or be destroyed, but nobody argues that such destruction should be considered in moral terms. We know perfectly well that matter in motion is not morally responsible for what it does, nor for the consequences that stem from its interactions with other material entities. Matter in motion is not moral or immoral, it is amoral—the category of morality simply does not apply in any coherent or rational way.

The assumptions of materialism

On the assumptions of materialism—and this is critical—*human beings are nothing more than matter in motion*. Everything about us reduces to material components. When someone punches someone else, matter in motion collides with another material entity and damage results. Given materialism, however, there is nothing that makes that interaction a moral interaction, any more than two meteors colliding is a moral interaction. Some atheists grant this, but others insist there really are relevant differences. For example, meteors do not have central nervous systems or the ability to feel pain. Since they can't experience pain, they can't be hurt, and therefore the destruction of a meteor does not violate their moral rights. This is true to a point, but insufficient. A tiger that successfully hunts a deer hurts it, but we don't judge that the tiger has done anything immoral. Even if a tiger becomes a maneater, we don't charge it with immorality. The morality of an event, therefore, cannot simply be chalked up to whether or not the victim endures pain.

Matter in motion, like a meteor for instance, is not morally responsible for what it does or the interactions it has—it is amoral. To put human beings in the same category seems intellectually absurd.

Another suggestion that materialists typically make is that the difference is one of personality, intention and rational thinking. Human beings deliberate about their actions and are responsible for them in a way that other material entities are not. Because people have the cognitive capacities required for purposeful decision-making, and the further ability to know what effects are likely to be produced by their actions, what we do can be judged as good or evil. According to this line of reasoning, the reason that human matter in motion is moral is tied to human intentions and intelligence.

This response is wholly inadequate for a number of reasons. One of the reasons is that it simply doesn't go deep enough in its analysis. Human beings think, plan and act on the basis of intentions. But what generates human thought? For a materialist, human thought is produced by nothing more than the physical brain. Needless to say, the physical brain is nothing more than matter in motion. It is the cobbled-together product of blind evolutionary forces. According to many leading Darwinians, the human brain was shaped through countless positive adaptive mutations that conferred survival advantage on the organisms that were lucky enough to mutate in such positive ways. This physical organ controls the physical organism. It is matter in motion controlling matter in motion. This means that every single thought the brain produces is generated from non-sentient, non-self-conscious, non-intelligent, whirring little atoms. In materialism, all human *thinking* comes from matter in motion.

How can people be held morally responsible for their conduct, if what they do is nothing more than the result of the matter in motion inside of their head? DNA constructed their brains, and it is very difficult to see how people can be responsible for what their DNA does (or what their parents' DNA does in them, if you will). People have no control over the atoms and electro-chemical interactions that constitute their brains—how can they somehow become morally responsible for what these chemical interactions cause their physical bodies to do? The brain regulates our moods and our nervous system and our muscle movements and our bodily functions. If the brain causes our arm to move through space and strike another body, it is sheer category jumping to say that such an interaction of two material bodies is part of the moral domain. As has been often said, given materialism, the brain secretes thought like the liver secretes bile. How is secreted thought a proper foundation for morality? In a materialistic order, there is nothing that can lift human beings out of the purely amoral condition of matter in motion.

On the local level of the human organism, then, the concept of morality is inapplicable, because all human behaviour is nothing more than matter in motion and the result of matter in motion. A massive entailment of this is that human beings are not—indeed, cannot be—responsible for what they do. If all human action arises from physical-chemical-electrical interactions over which we have no conscious control (and everything we associate with our conscious realm is really beyond our control in this model), then all of our emotions, dispositions, ideas, thoughts, intentions, judgements, decisions and actions *are things that happen to us and in us.* I have no control over whether my brain puts into effect a chain of sequences that results in my punching someone, stealing their things, giving them a present or risking my life for them. If responsibility and control are required for moral behaviour—which they are—then materialism precludes moral action. We do things, but we do not do things morally, nor do we do moral things—morality simply doesn't apply.

On a broader level, it is also worth noting that the nature of a materialistic universe makes the very concept of morality unintelligible. Not only are human beings not moral beings, and not only are we not capable of moral action, morality itself is very problematic in a naturalistic order. Morality, of course, is not comprised of matter. When we ask about "goodness" we are not asking about a particular lump of molecules. Does "goodness" and "evil" emerge only when matter interacts with other matter in certain ways? Some materialists try to find a home for goodness or "the good" as a timeless, unchanging abstraction. But it's difficult to demonstrate persuasively that an abstraction has any type of independent existence apart from minds. How did "goodness" exist when there was nothing? It is one thing to say that "goodness" has somehow just existed eternally as an abstract standard, but this is hardly very consistent with the metaphysics of a naturalistic worldview. It amounts to special pleading. Was being unkind to children really objectively immoral before anything existed? What kind of existence could moral standards have when they were alone in a sea of nothingness?

The types of concerns found in the last paragraph are the subjects of seemingly interminable debate.[1] They cannot be profitably pursued here. What is worth noticing, however, is that materialists have a very real problem even if we grant that goodness has some kind of actual

---

[1] The great divide between the philosophies of Plato and Aristotle was based on similar issues. Medieval philosophy was also characterized by astonishingly subtle debates on the nature of abstract entities. For those centuries, the nominalists and the realists fiercely disagreed about these matters. Perhaps it is safe to say that contemporary debates are not as rhetorically charged and emotionally heated, but philosophers still tend to sort out into the broad camps of either the Platonists or the Aristotelians.

ontological or metaphysical status as a timeless, abstract principle. On a practical level, it boggles the imagination to think that good and evil exist as abstract, eternal moral categories, and then a universe came into existence out of nothing, matter collided with matter, and over time this matter became self-conscious and somehow *figured out the true nature of these immaterial moral standards*! The odds of such a thing are incalculable. To think that fragments of matter would bind together and then get in touch with these abstract standards, especially when matter and morality constitute completely separate types of realities, is a narrative that seems to depend on blind faith and incredulity.

When we add that the evolutionary process aims at survival no matter what the costs (which is the diametric opposite of principles of morality), we have to realize that the process by which matter allegedly attained the ability to identify these timeless moral standards is aimed in *exactly the opposite direction from the content of these moral standards*.

Roughly speaking, the evolutionary process is selfish, but morality is selfless. Abstract moral standards are mute—they could never communicate to people. But neither could matter in motion somehow reach up to them, and find communion with these eternal, immaterial, abstract standards of good and evil. So, besides the *metaphysical* problem, there exists the *pragmatic* problem: Why would we think that unguided matter in motion *accidentally figured out the true nature of eternal, objective morality*?

Furthermore, it is absurdly mind-boggling to think that these eternal, abstract standards are exactly the principles that *happen to be most conducive to the continued survival of an evolved species inhabiting a material universe that came into existence out of nothing*. How could evolved brains learn eternity's moral code, and how could that abstract, eternal code just happen to be the single best guide for their physical survival?

An incoherent ethical system

There is more to say. Since the time of the skeptic David Hume, it has rightly been recognized (by many) that an ethical *ought* cannot be derived from a material *is*. Science is *descriptive*: it observes and describes what is. Science is not *prescriptive*: it is not able to say what *ought to be* in an ethical sense. A witness can see and describe a robbery, but they do not directly see the morality of the act. A moral judgement represents *how we evaluate* an event—it is our *response* to what we observe, and therefore cannot be part of what we actually observed in the first place. Scientists, therefore, can describe what *is*, but this does not legitimize the move from describing what one observed to passing moral judgements about what should or should not have been observed. (Given materialism all human behaviour is determined, so pontificating about what *ought* to be done is entirely pointless anyway. In fact, even our moral evaluations are determined.) The claims "that caused pain" and "it is wrong to cause unnecessary pain" belong to completely different realms of analysis. Materialists have no way of bringing these spheres together.

David Hume (1711-1776) was a Scottish philosopher who is known for his empiricism and skeptical views. He believed that moral claims were more psychological than rational.

Some consistent atheists have accepted the fact that materialism and morality cannot be held together in any consistent fashion. Some have argued that morality is a figment of our imagination, and that all things are equally amoral. This position is anarchic and destroys all moral value. (I suspect it is also fraudulent. There are a few who like to talk this talk, but I don't know anyone who consistently walks this walk.) In the end, this position entails that torturing and molesting orphaned children is morally equivalent to feeding them. Nobody really believes this is true, and nobody lives it out. If someone tries to make a show by insisting they see no moral difference between raping a child and building a hospital, they are worth pitying, but not debating. Moral values can be verbally denied by sophists, but it is impossible for us to live without them.

Those seeking a refuge in moral relativism or subjectivism—if consistent—will find that their position leads in a straight logical line back to the dead-end of moral nihilism (i.e. the view that morality is really nothing, that moral claims are meaningless, and that nothing can be more or less moral than anything else). If moral values and ethical judgements are nothing more than arbitrary community standards, or the subtle workings of will to power, or an illusion foisted on us by our genes—or whatever else—then we don't have objective morality. This will bring us back to *moral nihilism*. But moral nihilism is untenable. It is *profoundly* untenable. It may be one of the most untenable theories ever proposed in the long history of human thought. But it is the moral theory that coheres the best with the metaphysics of materialism. Given materialism, moral nihilism is the rational ethical choice. A rational analysis of naturalism leads to an irrational ethical system. Conversely, it is irrational for a materialist to have a rational ethical system. When rationality leads to irrationality, the worldview as a whole is incoherent.

CHRISTIANITY AND VALUE

Objective morality is rooted in God's character

In contrast to naturalism, Christian theology and morality are organically connected. Morality is not merely compatible with Christianity, it is an integral part of it. God's universe is *intrinsically* a moral order. There is not merely a moral *dimension* to the universe. Morality is woven into the very fabric of creation. Human beings are moral beings who have moral knowledge and make moral judgements on the basis of an objective moral standard. This standard is not abstract and impersonal, but concrete and personal. The standard of moral goodness is the perfect character of a holy and loving God. In God, fact and value, *is* and *ought*, are merged in an eternally coherent relationship. Morality is rooted in God's character and flows from him. Since the universe is his creation, and since human beings are his image bearers, people cannot escape his objective moral demands. God is the standard of goodness, the one who issues moral commands and imperatives, and the one who holds people accountable for the good and evil for which they are responsible. In the Christian worldview, morality is intelligible, it is objective and it is undeniable. As we have seen, people cannot cogently deny the existence of moral reality, and materialism as a worldview cannot provide

> **In the Christian worldview, morality is intelligible, it is objective and it is undeniable.**

a coherent account of morality's place either in the universe or in human experience.

Beauty—physical, spiritual and ethical

It is not only morality that belongs in the Christian worldview: God's creation and revelation is also the true home of beauty. Naturalistic evolution devalues beauty and makes it the subjective, accidental by-product of self-conscious genetic units. In this model, intrinsic beauty is absurd. Furthermore, the evolutionary process is a very unlikely pathway to the discovery of the beautiful—there is no *survival advantage* attached to being transported into a realm of wonder and awe. Marvelling at a sunset or staring at the Milky Way is not likely to help you pass on your genetic material. In fact, being distracted and captivated by aesthetic sensibilities is more likely to make you vulnerable to predators and oblivious to dangers. Standing in awe and appreciation before majestic beauty is very, very surprising given naturalism. It is one thing to identify a potential mate. Thinking that a sunset is gorgeous is another thing entirely. How strange to imagine that a universe came into existence out of nothing, matter in motion collided with matter in motion, the matter became self-conscious and then the matter developed the capacity to marvel at the beauty it perceived in matter. This marvelling had no intrinsic survival purpose—it was merely a by-product of mutations that aided genetic reproduction.

In the Christian view of things, God is not only a being of exquisite, pure beauty, he is the *Source* of all beauty. He is perfectly balanced in his nature. Everything he is fits together in perfect harmony, so much so that he is a simple being. God is also infinitely pleasing. When God created the universe, he constructed it to reflect his beauty, and he designed human beings to be able to recognize, appreciate and delight in aesthetics. This reality points us beyond the material realm to the spiritual one. God, of course, does not have beauty because of physical symmetry, spatial proportions or pigmentation. The universe, however, is a material analogue: beauty in the physical sphere is a revelation of the beauty of God. Beauty in our universe points beyond itself to its Source.

Even more important, our universe is also a place where we find spiritual and ethical beauty. When we see someone full of hatred and bitterness, we see spiritual and ethical ugliness. This ugliness, however, presupposes that there is a positive standard, an ethical ideal. Ugliness has no independent existence apart from beauty. When we see self-sacrificing love, or genuine humility, or selfless compassion or heartfelt forgiveness, we are struck by its fundamental rightness and beauty. When someone does something especially selfless and pure, we often encourage them by saying something along the lines of, "That was a *beautiful* thing you did." Beauty and morality are fraternal twins. Through the medium of our physical actions in this physical world, we have the opportunity to express moral and spiritual beauty. We also have the opportunity to make the world an ugly place, cause pain and deform our characters. Nevertheless, even the most morally stunted—those who have shouted down their ethical sensibilities—still tend to recognize intuitively the rightness of the beautiful.

Since this is part of the fabric of the universe, and since we are designed as aesthetic beings, it is not surprising that we are enraptured by beauty. God's creation is a revelation—it always reveals his glory. Marvelling at a sunset is not an end in itself—the streaking colours of the sky point beyond themselves to the artist who envisioned them and gave them life. John Calvin said that this universe is a theatre where the glory of God is displayed. He was absolutely right. We could also add that this world is an art gallery, a concert hall, a dance studio and a matchless piece of prose-poetry (*prosetry*, if you like).

Archetypes

As the image bearers of God, we are able to recognize and appreciate beauty, and we are also able to produce it. Students of literature have long noted that in works that are cross-culturally appreciated, certain themes come up again and again. There are certain ideas that resonate deep within people, regardless of their language, culture or even their time in history. Carl Jung identified the fact that all over the world, human beings are moved by the same archetypal concepts. These archetypes shape our understanding of the world, and they also allow us to interpret the world in meaningful ways. They are embedded in humanity's collective unconscious. Over time these archetypes can be consciously identified and analyzed, but they are already present in the human psyche.

Where do these archetypes come from? They are not explicitly taught, nor are they merely imbibed from society. How can we account for their universal distribution? The biblical account tells us that the first humans were once placed in a pristine setting that was specially crafted by God. The Garden of Eden did not encompass the planet, but was one very small geographic part of it. This beautiful spot was lost because of human rebellion. As a result, human beings became guilty of rebellion against God. One of the results of their rebellion is that people labour under the echoing memory of Eden, trying to recover it, but living in a world marked by alienation and futility. Yet there remains an archetypal memory of a golden age and a sense of loss. We live longing to regain the former state from which our ancestors fell, and in our hearts we feel the angst of guilt and fear, the need for reconciliation and forgiveness and the desire for redemption. Deep down, we know there is no going back. There is only one direction we can go, and that is forward. As a result, we can't live without a hope for the future.

We find that great art connects with these themes. Some pieces of art focus narrowly on one aspect, one archetype. For example, some art is hideous, but it is still good art because it shows the reality of ugliness. Depictions of violence, lust, anarchic rebellion, greed and chaos should not provoke imitation. On the contrary—staying true to Aristotle's meaning of *catharsis*—the presentation of evil and ugliness should lead to revulsion and help purify us from any desire to defile ourselves with the things depicted.

Art can inspire us *toward* the beautiful, but it can also be effective in leading us *away* from impurity. Being brought face-to-face with evil in all of its stark ugliness will cause a moral person to turn away from it, and even strengthen their resolve to fight against it. If a virtuous person watches a movie that realistically depicts the struggle of minorities against racial hatred and violence, they will be horrified. Far from moving closer toward racism, they will be repelled. In fact, seeing a vivid depiction of the ugliness of racism can help to combat it. Art can help us appreciate beauty, even if it sometimes does so by showing us beauty's negation.

Due to the nature of literature, writing is one of the most natural mediums in which to explore and embrace these archetypes. Fiction writers are able to construct narratives that develop these universal themes in poignant ways that connect with our minds, hearts and souls. As literary geniuses, J.R.R. Tolkien and C.S. Lewis clearly understood that their fantasy works were appealing to mass audiences because they drew on religious and emotional archetypes. In fact, they argued that all great mythology reflected biblical themes. Beyond this, they suggested that the archetypal themes that are found in literature and mythology were related to God's grand narrative of creation, redemption and re-creation. They believed that the archetypes expressed in mythology resonated within human hearts, because all people are primed to long for the fulfillment of these archetypal desires.

Longing for ultimate fulfillment

Literature and mythology touch on the archetypes, but leave us hungering and thirsting for more. The satisfying of our hunger and the quenching of our thirst, however, is found in only one place: the greatest story of them all, the gospel of Jesus Christ. In the gospel, the poignant truths that are represented in mythology come into time and space history, our deepest human needs are met, there is ultimate fulfillment and the greatest good emerges from the greatest darkness. The themes of great literature inspire and enrich us because they are inseparably related to God's deepest purposes for us and the universe. In mythology, we hear whispers of the gospel, and in the gospel we find the converging together of all our individual archetypical longings. Unlike mythological figures and other characters in literature, Jesus was a historical person. In God's narrative, myth and history are fused. They were always meant to be.[2]

We still await the ending of this first act in God's great drama. The Redeemer has come, died as our Substitute and has been raised to life forevermore. Even though we have not yet reached the historical consummation of God's story, we are being pointed toward it. We find that nothing in this world is completely fulfilling. We find that in our moments of most profound joy there is an emptiness, a lack, an ineffable something missing. We grope for it but it is just, *just* out of reach. The reason why, of course, is that this world is not our final home. What we really long for is heaven. We have been designed to long for God.

Engaging with the arts can stir up our desire for God. Many people

---

[2] The word myth, of course, does not in this context denote *fictitious*. It refers to *significance*. Myths are organizing interpretive narratives that try to make human experience intelligible. Many are fictitious, but that is irrelevant.

in our society are too distracted, too over-stimulated and too bored to pay much attention to the arts. This is quite sad. On the other extreme, there are people who are so serious and business-minded that they miss out on the fact that the arts are not only elevated, they are elevating. They have the potential to truly expand our capacities. For Christians, our goal is to maximize the glory of God and to delight in him. In order to delight in God, and savour him to the fullest extent of which we are capable, we need to stretch and grow and train our faculties.

This is something that Andrew Rozalowsky experienced during the very last month of his earthly life. I walked into his hospital room mere weeks before he died, and there on his bedside was C.S. Lewis' *Space Trilogy*. Before then, I had never seen anyone reading a copy of it, nor did I have any idea that he had one. This was a delightful moment of serendipity—just a few days prior, I had ordered a copy of the exact same book. In fact, when I got back to my office after our visit, I found that my copy of the *Space Trilogy* had been delivered while I was with him. During our visit, we discussed Lewis and literature and Christianity. We said we'd start a book club, and the *Space Trilogy* was first on our list. Although Andrew did not live long enough to finish it, he wrote a very personal blog post about the value of this reading. He entitled it, "Fiction Changed Me (C.S. Lewis and God)":

C.S. Lewis (1898–1963) held academic positions at both Cambridge and Oxford universities. He was a scholar, literary critic, essayist, lecturer, Christian apologist and author, writing both fiction and non-fiction works.

I was wrong to ignore fiction so long.

I started off young as a reader, which set me on a good foot, but one of the laments I have of my adolescence is that I wasn't encouraged to continue being a reader. Sports and then music took over my life. I did the minimal in English classes (though I managed to score high— how?) and you'd be shocked at how few of the classics I've read. It wasn't until I became a Christian at age 20 when my newfound love of the Bible kindled in me a desire to read and learn in order to know God. This meant reading lots of non-fiction as I sought to learn the languages, culture, history, etc. of the Bible. It lead me into degrees in philosophy and biblical studies. All good.

But along the way fiction has played a small to minimal role in my life. I've justified myself by thinking it was of a second rate. Sure, it's a good hobby to have; something to unwind with; something for entertainment.

But I was wrong.

A couple weeks ago, as my mental strength returned inbetween chemo rounds, I picked up C.S. Lewis's Space Trilogy. From the first chapter of Out of the Silent Planet, *I was enthralled by his ability to write. And I mean write! His words were a joy to read and a story that starts out with a Cambridge philologist didn't hurt getting me into the narrative either!*

But something really changed in me as I kept reading and especially as I moved into and through Perelandra. *I started to see life differently and the romantic part of me came alive. It awakened imaginations and feelings about life that were seemingly suppressed down below. It has changed my thinking, my processing, my writing. There's no way I won't return to my academic studies a better thinker. There's no way I won't return to reading the Bible more romantically. That's already been the case day by day.*

Perhaps the greatest joy of this reading was Lewis's ability to magnificently retell the story of Eden, good and evil, temptation, Fall, Incarnation, redemption, and New Creation that most awakened in me greater praise to God. At first I thought Lewis was brilliant—and, well, he was. But then I came to see that really he understood God and the Bible so well (not to mention other classic literature), that he was able to tell the 'Old Story' in such a way that I have come back to the Bible with awakened eyes. It was me who was dead. Lewis helped me see beyond him, his writing, and his story to the magnificence of God and his marvelous creative and redemptive work. And here he used fiction to do it.

Andrew, despite leaving the trilogy unfinished, found that what he read lifted him up and made him more appreciative of beauty, purity and joy. It increased his aesthetic sensitivity. It served as a signpost, something that arrests attention in order to point beyond itself. We are to see the beauty before us so we can see the beauty beyond us. Earthly beauty points to heavenly beauty. Finite joy points to infinite joy. Creation points to the Creator. We have innate desires and longings, none of which can be satisfied in this temporal world. We know of not a single other innate desire that does not correspond to something that can fulfill it. As C.S. Lewis observed, we hunger and there is food, we thirst and there is drink. All of our innate longings have the potential of being fulfilled.

What are we to think when we find an innate desire for infinity, eternity and perfection? Simply put, we are to think that there is something that will fulfill that desire. Since it is not found in this world, it must be found in another. (Notice that we do not infer from our desire that there is heaven—that there is a heaven is revealed to us by God. But the revelation and the inference, the desire and the promise, are in one accord.) The gifts will not satisfy us. Our hearts can only find satisfaction in the Giver. We need the Source. *We need God.*

One of the most glorious realities of the Christian message is that Jesus Christ has secured for us the ultimate satisfaction of our holy, good and God-given longings for himself. When we arrive at the city we don't go back to stare at the road sign that points toward it. A picture of our loved ones can give us comfort when we are apart, but when we're together again we look at them rather than their picture. Beauty in art and literature points beyond itself to the True Beauty. When a believer is brought into the presence of Beauty, the signposts are no longer required. Reading the *Space Trilogy* may raise us to new heights in our appreciation of God's great redemptive story—at least in this world. But being raised to heaven...meeting Jesus...seeing God...being surrounded by beauty and infused with it...moral perfection...holy splendour—words fail.

> **Beauty in art and literature points beyond itself to the True Beauty.**

Even Lewis could not describe this—since he was brilliant, he didn't try. One of his most famous and well-loved sections in the *Chronicles of Narnia* describes the indescribability of the world to come. For Lewis, the end of the series is really the beginning. Aslan the Lion, the Christ-figure, speaks to the human protagonists, and gently explains to them that they died in a train accident on earth. Aslan says:

> "Your father and mother and all of you are—as you used to call it in the Shadowlands—dead. The term is over: the holidays have

begun. The dream is ended: this is the morning."

And as He spoke He no longer looked to them like a lion; but the things that began to happen after that were so great and beautiful that I cannot write them. And for us this is the end of all the stories, and we can most truly say that they all lived happily ever after. But for them it was only the beginning of the real story. All their life in this world and all their adventures in Narnia had only been the cover and the title page: now at last they were beginning Chapter One of the Great Story which no one on earth has read: which goes on forever: in which every chapter is better than the one before."[3]

It is amazing that our world—cursed as it is because of sin—is still so incredibly beautiful. But it is a beauty that is tragically tainted. It is not completely pure and pristine. We find both a fundamental rightness and an inescapable wrongness in our present experience. The creation itself groans and longs for redemption.[4] Nevertheless, it is a beautiful, valuable and profoundly moral order. It is also a sign. It signifies (*sign*-ifies) a greater, more beautiful, morally perfect reality. This world—and the lives lived therein—point to God. We were made to be at home, but this current order is not that final resting place. We were designed for glory. The place where we belong is in the world to come. Our home is God's home. Far better to be there than to be reading about it.

One day God's children will all be there. Some have already gone ahead, following the trail blazed by the Lord Jesus Christ. But one day all of God's people will be gathered into the arms of the Father and ushered into their eternal home. Then, for the first time, we will understand the deep nature of beauty, joy and moral goodness. At that time, in the presence of God, we will appreciate how special such things are. Following the imagery of Lewis—who was following the imagery of Plato—we will move from the shadows to the light, from the overflow to the Source. What then? Something inexpressible, indescribable, uncontainable and unimaginable. As saints of old used to say, what awaits is the *beatific vision*, seeing the pure beauty of God. And once we behold him, we will never desire to turn away.

---

[3] C.S. Lewis, *The Last Battle* (New York: HarperCollins, 1984), 228.
[4] See Romans 8:20–22.

CHAPTER 7: SUMMARY AND APPLICATION

REMEMBER

The Ten Commandments (est. *c*.1445 B.C.)
You shall have no other gods before me.
 You shall not make for yourself an image in the form of anything in heaven above or on the earth beneath or in the waters below....
 You shall not misuse the name of the Lord your God, for the Lord will not hold anyone guiltless who misuses his name.
 Remember the Sabbath day by keeping it holy.
 Honour your father and your mother, so that you may live long in the land the Lord your God is giving you.
 You shall not murder.
 You shall not commit adultery.
 You shall not steal.
 You shall not give false testimony against your neighbour.
 You shall not covet your neighbor's house. You shall not covet your neighbour's wife, or his male or female servant, his ox or donkey, or anything that belongs to your neighbour (Exodus 20:3–17).

REFLECT

1. Aristotle believed that a virtuous person grows in virtue throughout the course of their lifetime. Does Scripture agree with this position?

2. How do the writings and insights of J.R.R. Tolkien and C.S. Lewis reflect biblical themes and glorious truths?

3. Aslan says, "Your father and mother and all of you are—as you used to call it in the Shadowlands—dead. The term is over: the holidays have begun. The dream is ended: this is the morning." Is this the hope beating in your heart today? If so, why? If not, why not?

REJOICE

Jesus Lord, I'm captured by Thy beauty,
  All my heart to Thee I open wide;
Now set free from all religious duty,
  Only let me in Thyself abide.
As I'm gazing here upon Thy glory,
  Fill my heart with radiancy divine;
Saturate me, Lord, I now implore Thee,
  Mingle now Thy Spirit, Lord, with mine.

Shining One—how clear the sky above me!
  Son of Man, I see Thee on the throne!
Holy One, the flames of God consume me,
  Till my being glows with Thee alone.
Lord, when first I saw Thee in Thy splendor,
  All self-love and glory sank in shame;
Now my heart its love and praises render,
  Tasting all the sweetness of Thy name.

Precious Lord, my flask of alabaster
  Gladly now I break in love for Thee;
I anoint Thy head, Beloved Master;
  Lord, behold, I've saved the best for Thee.
Dearest Lord, I waste myself upon Thee;
  Loving Thee, I'm deeply satisfied.
Love outpoured from hidden depths within me,
  Costly oil, dear Lord, I would provide.

My Beloved, come on spices' mountain;
  How I yearn to see Thee face to face.
Drink, dear Lord, from my heart's flowing fountain,
  Till I rest fore'er in Thine embrace.
Not alone, O Lord, do I adore Thee,
  But with all the saints as Thy dear Bride;
Quickly come, our love is waiting for Thee;
  Jesus Lord, Thou wilt be satisfied.

8

What does love do?

Since the character of God is the standard of goodness, all value flows from him. All of God's acts are in harmony with his infinite goodness and moral perfection. God created this universe not only to be beautiful (like a painting or sculpture) but to be a home for moral beings making significant ethical decisions. There are objective moral laws that operate with the certainty of physical laws. Every person who has ever lived is guilty of breaking at least some of these particular moral standards.

Acting out of his love and grace, God redeems and saves people who have sinned against him and violated the moral order. Once a person is redeemed, however, they are called to *grow* in ethical purity. God saves people and then works to conform them to the ethical character of his Son, Jesus Christ. It is impossible for anyone to be saved by making themselves good enough to be accepted by God. This is a fundamental principle of Christianity. Salvation is a *gift* of God's grace, paid for by Jesus Christ—we do nothing to earn it or deserve it. Nobody goes to heaven on the basis of their own merit. In fact, people go to heaven despite their *de-*merit. It is Christ's merit alone that is sufficient, and his merit is only given to people who trust him and commit themselves to him. This total commitment is what the Bible means when it uses the word *faith*.

BEING CREDIBLE MESSENGERS

Another fundamental principle of Christianity, however, is that once people have had Christ's merit credited to their account, they are to advance and grow in goodness. The internal changes that God's grace is making in a person's heart will reveal themselves in external acts. Even though Christians will never be perfect in this life—far from it—there should be a general consistency between their profession of faith, their character and their lifestyle.

Sadly, there has never been a shortage of hypocrites among the members of the human race. (Hypocrisy, of course, doesn't only flourish in religious circles, but religious hypocrisy is the most damaging and tragic kind.) Political propaganda, cover-ups and scandals are so routine that most of it is simply ignored by an apathetic and burnt-out public. Corruption is so rampant—as is the dishonesty that attempts to hide it—that it has become part of the normal backdrop of our society. We may still get *angry* when we hear about such things, but we are never *surprised*.

On a smaller scale, everyone knows people who say one thing and do another, or, colloquially, someone who can "talk the talk" but can't "walk the walk." Jesus warned his disciples not to be like certain religious leaders who did not *practice* what they preached (Matthew 23:3). Jesus' words are a warning to his followers, and a warning to religious hypocrites everywhere: God sees through you. People hear your words but they also see what you do. The easiest person in the world to fool is yourself.

The receptivity people have toward a message can't be separated from the credibility of the messenger who delivers it. This can be either positive or negative. On the one hand, we tend to be more skeptical about things we hear from people who have track records of spinning the truth, exaggerating, leaving out relevant facts or outright lying. On the other hand, we tend to be far less skeptical about things we are told by those who have proven themselves to be honest, forthright and generally reliable. This truth is the foundation for the tale about the boy who cried wolf, as well as the basis of ten thousand parental lectures. Simply put, personal integrity is a huge factor in communication.

Integrity is not only communicated verbally—in fact, we instinctively know that actions speak louder than words. An abusive husband might swear that he would never do anything to hurt his wife, but his verbal testimony is meaningless in the light of her bruises. Nobody believes that politicians will fulfill their promises to cut taxes, because past experience has shown that such promises are almost always empty. It is far easier to talk a good game than to play one.

The connection between the credibility of a message and the character of the messenger is not lessened when the message is the good news of Jesus Christ. As a matter of fact, many non-Christians claim that one of the main reasons they have no interest in church is because of the hypocrisy of Christians. Now, this may be an excuse, and it may be an example of the fallacy of hasty generalization, but believers need to take seriously the fact that hypocrisy is often cited as a reason for ignoring the church's message. When the world is confronted with Christians who are angry and hateful, the gospel of grace and love is drowned out by the personal immorality of the messengers. This is one of the reasons why Peter urged his readers to be ready to give a reason for the hope that was within them, but to do so with gentleness and respect (1 Peter 3:15). Peter knew perfectly well that the message of hope will be either helped or harmed by the attitude, tone and character of the messengers.

It would be difficult to exaggerate the importance of this truth. If we are to be effective witnesses and apologists, we must cultivate a godly character. We must learn how to articulate the reason for our hope, but we must also grow in virtue and holiness. A message of grace can only be delivered effectively by a grace-filled, grace-dispensing individual who continually marvels at the saving grace of God in their own life. Likewise, a message of love cannot be delivered by a person who is filled with hate. Messages of peace are not sent by warmongers, nor are messages of wisdom fittingly put in the

> **A message of grace can only be delivered effectively by a grace-filled, grace-dispensing individual who continually marvels at the saving grace of God in their own life.**

mouths of fools. The most important message in the universe—the gospel of Jesus Christ—needs to be delivered and defended by Christ-like individuals. Actually, it is ultimately impossible to divide or split this holistic witness: the gospel message must be communicated by both Christ-honouring words and Christ-honouring lives. Only when there is harmony between head, heart and hands, will we be able to capably and persuasively defend the faith.

LOVE AND WITNESS

Loving one another

Shortly before his crucifixion, Jesus told his disciples that the world would be able to identify them by their love. Jesus said, "A new command I give you: Love one another. As I have loved you, so you must love one another. By this everyone will know that you are my disciples, if you love one another" (John 13:34–35). Jesus' instructions could not be simpler nor more important: people will recognize his disciples by their love for one another. The world may deny the truth of their message, but it cannot deny their love. A message of transforming love is hardly believable unless accompanied by the evidence of a transformed, loving life. Beyond this, the standard is impossibly high, apart from supernatural help: we are called to love one another the way Christ loved us. Christ's love for us led to his substitutionary, sacrificial death on the cross. We are to love each other no matter the cost, because this is what the Son of God did for us. Jesus' followers are called to imitate him. Christ's followers are called to love as Jesus loves.

Love is the crowning virtue of the Christian life, as well as its sum and substance. A life of love proclaims the reality of the gospel and also defends it. The best apologists will be full of the love of Christ. More people are impressed by a virtuous life than by intellectual brilliance and logical precision. We all know people who are intelligent, but also petty, tyrannical and arrogant. Far from being attracted to people like this, we are repelled by them and their message. Pride is repugnant, humility is attractive. Virtue outweighs intelligence. Actions speak louder than words.

First Corinthians 13 is a Bible passage that is often read at weddings. It beautifully and poetically extols the nature of love. It contrasts love with lesser things that—though outwardly impressive—are really worth nothing without love. For example, if we give away all of our possessions to charity, but don't love the people who will receive them, we aren't actually virtuous (1 Corinthians 13:3). Likewise, following a long list of religious rules and exercising tremendous self-restraint is meaningless in the sight of God unless we are full of love. There is not a single thing we can do that is even slightly virtuous unless we have love. The same is true of our words: nothing we say is of any value apart from love.

Paul is emphatic at this point. He writes, "If I speak in the tongues of men or of angels, but do not have love, I am only a resounding gong or a clanging cymbal. If I have the gift of prophecy and can fathom all mysteries and all knowledge, and have a faith that can move mountains, but do not have love, I am nothing" (1 Corinthians 13:1–2). This principle applies to our entire lives, but has a unique application in the task of apologetics. Even if we know everything, speak with flawless eloquence and always win the debate, it is all meaningless unless we love. No matter how brilliant, persuasive and compelling an apologist's arguments are, the apologist is *nothing* in God's estimation unless they are filled with holy love.

If the world will know that we are Jesus' disciples by our love, then the quality of our love must be one of our major concerns.

Often when we pray about our ministries and witnessing activities, we ask for success and increased abilities. We pray for wisdom, knowledge and the ability to witness effectively for the sake of Christ. We pray that God will open doors for the message, and we pray that we will have the insight and courage to walk through them in his power. We pray that God's Spirit will be at work to open hearts and minds. All of this is good, and we should pray along these lines, but we must not neglect praying for our *own* hearts. If the world will know that we are Jesus' disciples by our love, then the quality of our love must be one of our major concerns. Perhaps for some of us, the main problem we have in witnessing and defending the faith is not the depth of our knowledge nor the content of what we say—perhaps we are unfruitful because we lack love.

This can be approached from another direction. Perhaps our problem is that we are full of love, just the wrong kind. Perhaps we love *ourselves* more than we love *others*, or we love scoring points more than being gentle and respectful, or we love talking more than listening, or we love showing off how clever we are. (Attempting to show off your intelligence or education is one of the surest ways to convince people that you're a buffoon.) Perhaps we love "winning people to Christ" because it makes us feel useful, important, or—pathetically and perversely—it can even make us feel like we are holy and spiritually mature. We need to get rid of such attitudes. They must be put to death. Christ said that people will know that we are his followers by our love. The apostle Paul said that without love we gain nothing and are nothing. Yes, it is important that we pray for wisdom and the right words to say, but it is even more essential that we pray for love.

Loving God supremely

Love for people is rooted in love for God. When asked about the greatest commandments in the Old Testament, Jesus asserted that the greatest commandment was to, "Love the Lord your God with all your heart and with all your soul and with all your mind. This is the first and greatest commandment" (Matthew 22:37–38). Loving God is the most important thing in the universe. But after saying this, Jesus added, "And the second is like it: 'Love your neighbour as yourself.' All the Law and the Prophets hang on these two commandments" (Matthew 22:39–40).

> **Love for people is rooted in love for God.**

Unless we love God supremely we will not be able to love people properly. Love flows from the essence and nature of God—we can only love him because he loves us first. Furthermore, it is only when we adore God that we will be able to treat his image bearers as we ought. Loving God with all that we are is the greatest commandment, both in terms of importance and in terms of logical priority. In other words, loving God is the most important thing, but it is also what enables us to love other people deeply. If we are going to love others we must begin by loving God. It may not be said very often, but the best thing for witnessing to the world, proclaiming the gospel and defending the faith, is a deep, poignant, passionate, to-the-marrow, all-encompassing love for God.

It is this type of love for God that Andrew Rozalowsky displayed during his treatment and while he was on his deathbed. The reason his witness was so powerful was because he literally loved God more than his own life. (This is because, in part, he had discovered the truth of Psalm 63:3, that God's steadfast love for him was better than life.) Jesus Christ was more precious to Andrew than health, career, ministry and even other people. And he *loved* his family with a heroic intensity—he was never cold nor callous; in fact, his love for others shone brightest when his all-surpassing love for Christ was at its peak. Why was that? It was because, quite simply, loving God supremely doesn't diminish our love for others—it enhances and empowers it. We grow to love others more when we love God most. When I think of Andrew I remember his brilliance, wit and thoughtful comments. It is his character, however, that has left the deepest impression on me. It is his single-minded devotion to the glory of God. It is the profound trust he exhibited in the sovereignty of a loving God. It is his faith. It is his love.

Love is not a feeling

Biblical love is all-encompassing and all-transforming. We are to love God. We are to love our neighbours. We are to love our spiritual brothers and sisters. We are to even love our enemies. There is nobody who is excluded; there is nobody we get to hate. This does not mean that thinking about our enemies is supposed to produce warm and fuzzy feelings inside of us. Emotional feelings are not what love is about. This is one of the worst mistakes our society has made (and it has made many serious ones)—love is not a feeling.

When love is reduced to feelings, it is nothing more than covert selfishness. Someone makes us feel good and we like being around them, so we treat them well. It is possible that we may find that nothing makes us feel more valuable, or is as rewarding, as volunteering our time for charity. If this is the case, and unless we are very careful, giving to charity with our time and money can quickly become more about how it makes us *feel* than about *truly helping* those in need. If we get married because of how our partner makes us feel, what do we do when the feelings fade? Perhaps the catastrophic divorce rate in many societies goes part of the way toward supplying an answer.

If we are being honest, we all know that feelings come and go. Emotions change. Yes, emotions can grow stronger over time, and in many marriages and friendships they do. But if you listen to couples who have been happily married for more than a decade or two, you invariably hear them say that they didn't *feel* very loving during every moment of their married life. Deeply committed relationships usually look nothing like Hollywood romances. In real life, emotions don't burn brightly all the time. Honeymoon highs fade and marriage—as every couple and an army of marriage counsellors know—becomes something that requires work. If you marry someone because of how they make you feel, be aware that sometimes they will make you feel angry, hurt, sad, unappreciated, confused and even worse. They will certainly not always make you feel warm and elated and wonderful.

Faith in Christ inevitably bears fruit in a changed life. Especially in the area of our relationships, an unselfish, consistent, patient love is what will "speak" volumes to our family, friends and colleagues about what Jesus has done for us at the cross.

What often happens, sadly and destructively, is that when one spouse no longer feels like the other one is making them happy, they respond by punishing them with outbursts of anger, sullen withdrawnness, or the like. This, naturally, begins a downward spiral of relational misery. When we treat others well only when they treat us well, we will treat them poorly when we're not getting the emotional satisfaction from them that we want. If two people are in a relationship only because of how the other makes them feel, eventually the clash of competing self-centres will flare up in discord and dysfunction. Feelings are not only unstable, they are woefully inadequate as a foundation for intimate human relationships. If anyone doubts this, it is only because they have never taken a real look at the quality of the relationships that exist in our self-centred, emotionally driven society.

If we cannot reduce love to a feeling, then what is it? Love is a whole-hearted commitment to do what's best for someone else. It puts their needs ahead of your own. It endures all things for their sake. Love is an action; love is a deed. It is not based on what others have done to you, whether negative or positive. Love does not discriminate between people who make us feel good and people who make us feel badly. This is only possible because love is not feelings-based. The true nature of love is that it is actions-based. Selfishness asserts that you should make me feel good, and when you make me feel good I will act nicely toward you. In this approach, feelings come first and actions come second.

Whatever good we end up doing is contingent on our positive feelings. But this is a recipe for disaster, and it is not love. In real love, good actions are not dependent on our mood.

As a matter of fact, the priority and nature of real love is *exactly the opposite of the feelings-first model*. When there is real love, we act to bless other people, even if they don't repay us by making us feel good. Crucially, the actions are not done with the goal of feeling good, like a dog doing a trick hoping to receive a treat. Love works and does what's right, even if it's not appreciated, and even if there's no emotional payoff. Love is commitment and action. Ask couples who have been happily married for a long period of time what is more important: their day-by-day feelings or their lifetime commitment to each other. In a wonderful way, the couples with the deepest level of commitment are also the ones who attain the highest levels of happiness. This is because feelings don't lead to commitment: it is the other way around. Marital happiness is a by-product of commitment. Happiness is something you can never get if you're trying to get it. The surest way to be unhappy is to try to live your life with your *own* happiness as your goal. If anyone would save their life they must lose it, and if anyone loses their life they will find it.[1]

Once we begin to understand the nature of love, it becomes impossible to imagine that real love can be hidden or invisible. Nobody can see our feelings directly, although they may be able to infer them from our body language. People see actions. They hear what we say and see what we do. They also note what we don't do. In other words, love is displayed through our positive acts, and a lack of love can be displayed by both actions and neglect. Stealing someone's food causes direct harm; disinterestedly watching someone starve constitutes neglect. Both demonstrate a lack of love.

LOVE AT WORK

If the world will know that we belong to Christ because of our love, then it stands to reason that the world will be able to see Christians living a life of love. The love of God that is infused into the hearts of believers through the gospel of Jesus Christ cannot be hidden nor contained. When we fill up a glass with water, if we keep the water run-

---

[1] See Luke 9:24.

ning into the glass it starts to overflow. When capacity is exceeded, spillover always results. This is how it is with the love of God in the life of a believer. God's love begins to pour in, it fills us up and then it overflows. The overflow is seen in our actions.

The greatest act of all time, the greatest act of love in the history of the universe, was the sacrificial death of Christ on behalf of his enemies. He laid down his life to save those who hated him. God is love. Infinite love is revealed in historical action. As Christ loved us, so we are to love one another. Christ's love is not theoretical or ethereal. It is concrete and embodied. It is demonstrated. It is not a fuzzy feeling but a manifested sacrifice. It is self-giving and self-emptying. Christ poured himself out for others, taking their sin, penalty and death, so that they could receive eternal life. This is love. This is our pattern, source and motivation. We are to give as we have received. We are to bless as we have been blessed. Such a love cannot be covered up or hidden from sight. Genuine love is incarnate love—and incarnate love can be *seen*.

The link between our heart and our hands is not dissolvable. Throughout the history of the church, the church's witness has been strongest when it has demonstrated the love of Christ in word and in deed. Christians have fed the starving, clothed the naked, educated the illiterate, treated the sick, cared for orphans and fought against injustice. Despite attempts by some to demonize everything the church has ever done in history (Can we really take someone's judgement seriously when they claim that Christianity has produced nothing but negative effects throughout its entire history?), Christianity has had an enormously positive impact on the world. Yes, the institutional church has its share of guilt, abuse and sin. Still, many times what was called "the Church" was a corrupted political-economic institution that had nothing to do with following Jesus or the teachings of biblical Christianity. As a point of logic, the fact that some people falsely use the name of Jesus to mask their greed and exploitation of others, does not entail that there are no true followers of Jesus who selflessly loved, served and sacrificed for those in need. A false church does not rule out a true church any more than a counterfeit dollar rules out a genuine one.

In the following pages, I'm going to highlight just a few areas where Christians worked for the betterment of society, to correct injustice and to ensure basic human rights. The point is not to argue that the track record of the church's benevolence in history *proves* that it is an institution from God, but rather that the church—at its best—has endeavoured to follow Jesus in practical ways that effected positive change. The argument is not that non-Christians haven't done anything good or charitable and that Christians are all saints. All that is being claimed is that the witness of true believers has been—and should be—accompanied by social concern, love, mercy and sacrifice.

One more qualification needs to be made. (All these qualifications are wearisome, but so many people today seem unable to concede that the church hasn't "poisoned everything"; that if something can be interpreted in the worst possible way, it will be. Cynicism is neither an intellectual virtue nor a likely path to truth, but regrettably in some circles a biting, cynical stance toward everything "Christian" is taken as a sign of educational maturity.) I am fully aware that history is subject to vagaries and contingencies and multiple lines of causation. There are huge numbers of tangled, complex and complicated forces that rush together to generate various outcomes. With this in mind, I am not claiming that Christianity is the *sole* cause or that there are *no* other factors which impacted the following issues. By all means, let it be recognized that there are complexities—but by all means let it also be recognized that Christians, motivated by their religious convictions, were often the leaders in the fight for social justice in various spheres and at various times.

Christians have been instrumental in leading the charge against infant abandonment, exposure and murder.

1. Caring for the weak

In the Roman world in which Christianity was born, parents frequently abandoned their infants outdoors, leaving them to die from exposure. This was simply an accepted practice in society. This practice was only stopped when Christians began saving these abandoned infants and caring for them. They waged a war of love, using their scarce resources to take care of someone else's unwanted children. This love changed hearts and minds and eventually led to the abolishment of the practice. Exposing children (especially infant girls or twins) was also a common practice in China and parts of Africa before the gospel was introduced. Just like in the Roman world, it was the love of God displayed in the love of his followers that first challenged, then stopped, this practice of infant abandonment and murder. This is what love does.

In Western Europe, it was Christian love that led to the formation of our modern hospitals and hospices. Christians believed that the sick and dying should receive comfort and care, even though there was no economic benefit in alleviating the suffering of those who were about to die. During epidemics, it was the believers who tended to risk their own health by caring for the ill. All over the world there are hospitals, clinics and hospices that owe their existence to Christian principles. Many of the world's leading humanitarian organizations were founded on Christian ideals and were designed to share the love of Christ with the world in practical ways. Besides those organizations that were explicitly founded on Christian principles, the humanitarian impulse itself that flourishes in the Western World was originally grounded and rooted in Christian teachings.

This latter observation is incredibly important. It is enormously important that the ethical impulse of the West was not produced or grounded in a culture shaped by naturalistic atheism. Although there are disagreements about specific ethical issues, the wider ethical framework of the society in which Western atheists have been shaped is Judaeo-Christian. Atheists are influenced by the norms and values of their cultures as much as anyone else, and the norms and values of Western society have been deeply rooted in a broad ethic that was based on Scripture. Some atheists confidently like to assert that they live on the top floor of moral judgement, but the building they're occupying has a biblical foundation. Denying the existence of the foundation, or destroying it, is the surest way to bring down the entire structure.

The previous paragraph is hardly controversial. Bertrand Russell, the famed atheist, observed that Ghandi's policy of non-retaliation and pacifism only worked because, "…he was appealing to the conscience of a Christianized people."[2] This quotation adorns a museum dedicated to Ghandi in India. Why is it that a patriarch of modern atheism like Bertrand Russell can see what so many of his lesser followers scoff at? Why could he acknowledge that Ghandi's pacifism worked because the

---

[2] Quoted in Ravi Zacharias, *The End of Reason: A Response to the New Atheists* (Grand Rapids: Zondervan, 2008), 92.

British people were coming from a culture that had been shaped and grounded in a Christian ethic? What is the harm in admitting that Christianity has done a lot of good in the world, and that its influence goes beyond the activity of individual Christians? Notice that Russell is not arguing that Ghandi's strategy worked because he was dealing with *Christians*: he was arguing that it worked because Ghandi was dealing with a nation of people who had been *influenced societally* by Christian ethical principles.

2. The dignity of women

The very first thing the Bible says about the sexes is that both male and female are created *equally* in the image of God (Genesis 1:27). Paul insists that in salvation there is no difference between male and female (Galatians 3:28). In the New Testament, husbands are commanded to love their wives as Christ loved the church, dying for them and putting their needs above their own (Ephesians 5:25–33). As we saw in a previous chapter, Jesus' first post-resurrection appearances were to women rather than to his male disciples. Rodney Stark, a sociologist and historian, has conducted a meticulous study of the growth of the early church, and his findings are that, "Women in the early Christian communities were considerably better off than their pagan and even Jewish counterparts."[3] He notes that the early church had a very high percentage of women converts, and he concludes that one of the reasons for this is the fact that the church recognized the value of women in a way that completely transcended the view of the societies in which the church was born. Stark comments: "Women were especially drawn to Christianity because it offered them a life that was so greatly superior to the life they otherwise would have led."[4]

> **...the church recognized the value of women in a way that completely transcended the view of the societies in which the church was born.**

---

[3] Rodney Stark, *The Triumph of Christianity: How the Jesus Movement Became the World's Largest Religion* (New York: HarperOne, 2011), 122.

[4] Stark, *The Triumph of Christianity*, 122.

In the context of world religions, the place where women have the most freedom and dignity is in Christianity. Women are considered inferior to men in Hinduism. Hinduism still insists on the dehumanizing caste system—a system that the gospel of Jesus Christ renders unthinkable. In the caste system, the lowest of the low are the females who live at the bottom rung—the Dalits, those who are oppressed and untouchable. The extreme Hindu practice of *Sati* (widow-burning) is one of the more shocking symptoms of Hinduism's regard for women.

The plight of countless women in the Islamic world has been courageously exposed by Ayaan Hirsi Ali, a former Muslim who is now a self-proclaimed atheist. She reveals that women are entirely subjugated to their men and that the Islamic world is full of oppression and even violence against women (including so-called honour killings and genital mutilation). Ayaan is not a Christian, but she recognizes that in countries that are based on Christian values and ethics there is more freedom and dignity for women than what is found in Islamic nations.

3. Education

Christian truth also led to the establishment of our modern universities. Although they are currently far from their roots, the universities of Oxford, Cambridge, Harvard, Yale and Princeton (to name only a few) were all established with the express purpose of glorifying God and providing a place where people could discover more about his truth. The very idea of a university was that it would be a place where all subjects could be brought together into a coherent whole. A *uni*-versity is a place where diversity coheres in unity. Such unity in diversity is only possible if the totality of the universe is coherent, and we have the capacity to learn about it. Our greatest Western universities (and virtually all the rest, up until relatively recently) were founded on the principle that their very existence was only possible on the basis of the Christian worldview. They were established to teach and explore the nature of God and the nature of his created order. It was well understood that apart from Christianity a university would be a contradiction in terms. Our current society, and the enormous fissures that exist between academic departments that share a campus, has only served to justify what our pioneers in education knew: Christianity can give you a university, but anything less will only generate cognitive dissonance and disunity.

In church history, Christians were not only concerned with higher education. Christianity was the driving force behind the founding and organization of universal public education for children. It was believed that God's image bearers should not be illiterate. Furthermore, since God spoke through his Word, people needed to be capable of reading. Children needed to be taught so that they could flourish in God's world. Instead of worrying exclusively about the education of their own children, Christians wanted to see *all* children learn how to read and write. This desire is what lies behind the institution of Sunday school. Originally, Sunday school began as a school that met on Sundays, where Christians volunteered their time to teach children the basic skills of literacy.

4. Slavery

Christians were not only the driving force behind many good social developments, they were also the driving force behind the eradication of many evil ones. A special word needs to be said about slavery. Although space precludes anything approaching a full treatment of the topic, it is still worth making a few preliminary points.

Aiming at the heart

First, during the time of the New Testament, Christians were a tiny segment of the population with no political power. Slavery in the Greco-Roman world was part of the culture and a massive cog in the economic system. Directly opposing it would have been futile. The church could only begin to change society slowly, and the only way it could change society was to change *individuals* in society. The biblical message was aimed at the heart, with the understanding that when hearts were changed, actions and relationships would change, too.

Speaking directly to slaves

Second, the apostle Paul is the first writer in history to *directly address* slaves. Other writers would tell masters how they should manage their slaves, but Paul speaks to the slaves themselves. He addresses slaves as people with full value and dignity. Paul writes to Christians, and some Christians were slaves who had accepted the gospel. Since Paul had no clout with their masters, he had to help slaves learn to live in a way that was pleasing to the Lord, recognizing that there wasn't likely very much they could do to immediately change their circumstances. If Paul had written to converted slaves to tell them that they were free and no longer enslaved, he would only have caused trouble for them. If they listened to him, they would have been severely punished, and perhaps even put to death.

Speaking to masters
Third, Paul's instructions to masters are often overlooked. He writes, "Do not threaten [your slaves], since you know that he who is both their Master and yours is in heaven, and there is no favoritism with him" (Ephesians 6:9). In a similar context, Paul says, "Masters, provide your slaves with what is right and fair, because you know that you also have a Master in heaven" (Colossians 4:1). We need to notice that Paul presents masters as having *duties and obligations* to their slaves. Positively, they must provide fairly for their slaves. Negatively, they are not to threaten their slaves. Logically, if masters have to refrain from *threatening* their slaves, then masters will not be *beating or harming* their slaves. Most importantly, Paul places masters and slaves on the same plane—they both have the same Master in heaven to whom they are accountable. God will judge them without any favouritism (i.e. their social status is irrelevant). This is in perfect agreement with Paul's statement, "There is neither Jew nor Gentile, neither slave nor free, nor is there male and female, for you are all one in Christ Jesus" (Galatians 3:28). In the gospel, all sociological categories are transcended. *Everyone is equal in Christ.*

A concrete situation
Fourth, besides these instructions, we have one short letter from Paul that shows how he dealt with slavery in one concrete situation. A slave named Onesimus had run away from his master Philemon, who was a good friend of Paul's. Paul sends Onesimus back, carrying Paul's letter to Philemon. In the letter, among other things, Paul refers to Onesimus as his *son* (Philemon v. 10) and his *heart* (v. 12). Paul says he would love to have Onesimus stay with himself, but he is sending him back so that Philemon can receive him "no longer as a slave, but as a dear brother" (v. 16). Paul tells Philemon to welcome Onesimus as if he were Paul himself (v. 17). (How warmly would we expect Philemon to welcome his dear friend, the apostle?) Paul says he will personally pay

back anything Onesimus owes (v. 18). Then Paul adds that he is confident that Philemon will obey these instructions—and not only this, he will do more than has been asked of him (v. 21).

There is nothing from the Greco-Roman world that even approaches this. Once Christian principles were put into place—and once hearts were changed—slavery as an oppressive institution would die a natural death. When masters were taught to treat their slaves the way they would treat the apostles, and when they were to think of them as *brothers* rather than slaves, and when they remembered they all had the same Master in heaven…slavery could simply not survive.

The African slave trade
And that is exactly what happened. The African slave trade in the Western World was an abomination. Unlike slavery in the Greco-Roman world, it was based on racism. Unlike slavery in the Greco-Roman world, there was little possibility of ever gaining freedom. (In the Greco-Roman world, many slaves gained their freedom in their 30s, and becoming free was a reasonable expectation for most.) The African slave trade was also based on kidnapping and human trafficking, something that is explicitly forbidden in the Bible (1 Timothy 1:10). An honest reading of Scripture and an honest assessment of the African slave trade will show that they are completely incompatible.

It is not surprising, then, that the abolition of this institution was brought about by the tireless efforts of Christians. William Wilberforce was a British politician who, because of his evangelical convictions, waged a political war against the slave trade. Part of his inspiration came from a man named John Newton (the author of the hymn, "Amazing Grace").

William Wilberforce (1759–1833) campaigned tirelessly, over many years, for the abolition of the African slave trade. Transformed by conversion in 1784, he later wrote in his journal, "God Almighty has set before me two great objects, the suppression of the Slave Trade and the Reformation of Manners [moral values]."

Newton was a former slave trader and slave ship captain who converted to Christ and became an outspoken opponent of slavery on the basis of the Bible's teachings. Interestingly, early on, Wilberforce doubted that being a politician was a useful way to spend one's life, and he thought about becoming a preacher. He went to visit Newton and told him that he was thinking about leaving politics to enter pastoral ministry. Newton strongly insisted that he stay in politics with the goal of fighting against the slave trade and bringing it to an end. Wilberforce listened to Newton and spent the next decades trying again and again in Parliament to pass legislation outlawing the slave trade. It was only because of his Christian convictions that he persevered through insult, animosity and the repeated defeats of his bills. In the end, the most powerful force in England fighting against slavery was Wilberforce, and behind Wilberforce was a former slave captain who had converted to Christianity and who believed the slave trade must be stopped because it was evil in the sight of God.

On both sides of the Atlantic, the leaders in the battle against slavery were motivated by their Christian beliefs. This is a historical fact. The Western slave trade was abolished because of vocal Christian leaders who refused to put political expediency and economic gain ahead of human freedom. They did this because of the *gospel*; they did this because of the New Testament. Without Christianity, the driving force behind the abolition of slavery in the Western World would have been missing. If it wasn't for Christianity, there is no reason to believe that slavery would not have continued for decades (or centuries), or that it would not still be institutionalized and enforced in the Western World. It is easy to say that it *just wouldn't be*, but there is little evidence to bolster that happy optimism. If you remove the driving force, why think you'd still inevitably produce the same result? Remember Russell's thought about Ghandi: we are so indebted to the positive ethic of a Christianized people that the roots of the moral stands we take are often overlooked or taken for granted. But if the root wasn't there, why is it rational to expect to find the same fruit?

5. The fruit of love
Social justice and social activism are just some of the ways that Christians show the love of God to the world, and in so doing proclaim and defend the faith. On a smaller scale, individual Christians should be known for doing thousands of small kindnesses that bless others. If the gospel is put into practice, a believer's internal transformation will be manifested in external activity. A changed heart leads to loving deeds done with active hands.

But this great potential for showing the love of Christ to the world is also what makes the church vulnerable to the charge of hypocrisy. In other words, when people claim to follow Christ but then act in ways that are contrary to his teaching, the truth of the gospel is not defended, it is called into question. If your neighbour claims to be a Christian but then robs you, something is amiss, something is false. Unfortunately, in our society people seem to assume immediately that the *gospel* is false, rather than considering the possibility that the person's *claim to follow Jesus* is false. Jesus himself makes it perfectly clear that some people will say they believe in him, but their actions will prove that they are not his disciples.

Failure to live as Jesus instructed has done immense damage to the witness of the church. Hypocrites with false professions are confused for genuine believers. Before a watching world, genuine believers also fall short of Christ's standards, sometimes tremendously. Christianity has been confused with politics, institutions, organizations and even societies. (As much as a nation can be "Christianized" or *influenced* by Christian principles, an actual "Christian nation" has never existed, and never can exist: Christ's church transcends national boundaries—it does not create new ones.)

In the Western World, too often what was known as "the church" was more of a political institution than a group of people loving God and following Jesus. Unfortunately, this corruption of the church and distortion of the gospel is what many people think of when they think about Christianity. As a result, the hypocrisy, immorality, violence, greed and deep-rooted corruption of a church-that-isn't-the-church becomes one of the reasons people have for rejecting the gospel. We need to avoid the fallacy of equivocation: the one word *church* can mean very different things depending on context. It is not disingenuous to insist that what is often labelled "the church" is the opposite of what "the church" is. One lesson, however, is crystal clear: when Christ's followers act like Christ, the work of their hands supports their verbal witness. On the flipside, when people claim to follow Christ but their profession is contradicted by the work of their hands, those who know them are turned off the gospel.

> **...when Christ's followers act like Christ, the work of their hands supports their verbal witness.**

Ultimately—and to be fair—we must always return to the question of what Jesus himself actually did, and what he actually taught his disciples. Not everyone who claims to follow Christ, actually follows Christ, nor does anyone follow Jesus perfectly. If we are to judge an action's compatibility with Christian principles, we need to return to what Jesus actually said. The standards of the Bible are what count. We have every right to look at what people do and compare their actions to the teachings of Scripture. This is the true test for biblical ethics.

Still, as has often been noted, most people in society are not going to read the Bible to discover what Jesus really said. What they will read is your life. The impression they will have of the gospel will be correlated with their impression of you. God help us—literally. Only God can help us to live our lives in a way which makes the gospel sweet and attractive to others.

God needs to work in them, but he also needs to work in us. Our hearts need to change so that our actions can change. We always act in accordance with our character: a godly character produces godly fruit, and an ungodly character produces ungodly fruit. Gospel change occurs *internally*, but it can't help but be manifested *externally*. God transforms our hearts, and in so doing he transforms our hands. Since people can't see inside of us, the strength of our witness and defence of the faith will hinge on how we live. Perhaps it is time for all apologists to see how Paul's statement that, "The only thing that counts is faith expressing itself through love" (Galatians 5:6b) applies to the practice of apologetics.

CHAPTER 8: SUMMARY AND APPLICATION

REMEMBER

> Love is patient, love is kind. It does not envy, it does not boast, it is not proud. It does not dishonor others, it is not self-seeking, it is not easily angered, it keeps no record of wrongs. Love does not delight in evil but rejoices with the truth. It always protects, always trusts, always hopes, always perseveres. Love never fails.... And now these three remain: faith, hope and love. But the greatest of these is love (1 Corinthians 13:4–8a,13)

REFLECT

Biblical apologetics requires a changed life: head, heart, hands and feet. This transformation impacts our entire life and outlook. The author has demonstrated how Christianity impacts society. Consider:

1. How are you seeking to practice caring for the weak—those with physical, emotional and mental health issues? Are there any God-given opportunities to do so?

2. How we treat one another as image bearers reflects our love to God. Yet women are still exploited and abused especially in third world countries. The gospel is the answer. What action should we take, if any?

3. Education is a privilege not only for the elite, but for all humankind. The gospel actively liberates minds as well as hearts. The gospel is the answer. What action should we take, if any?

4. Sex slavery is soaring in the twenty-first century. Other forms of bondage remain, such as the Hindu caste system. The gospel is the answer. What action should we take, if any?

5. Our prayer is that this book may help better equip you to declare

and defend your faith and hope to your family and friends through a Christlike life.

REJOICE

To God be the glory, great things He has done;
  So loved He the world that He gave us His Son,
Who yielded His life an atonement for sin,
  And opened the life gate that all may go in.

Praise the Lord, praise the Lord,
  Let the earth hear His voice!
Praise the Lord, praise the Lord,
  Let the people rejoice!
O come to the Father, through Jesus the Son,
  And give Him the glory, great things He has done.

O perfect redemption, the purchase of blood,
  To every believer the promise of God;
The vilest offender who truly believes,
  That moment from Jesus a pardon receives.

Great things He has taught us, great things He has done,
  And great our rejoicing through Jesus the Son;
But purer, and higher, and greater will be
  Our wonder, our transport, when Jesus we see.

—Fanny J. Crosby (1875)

Fanny Crosby (1820–1915) was a prolific hymnwriter, having composed almost 9,000 hymns. Blind since shortly after birth, Crosby is considered the "mother of modern congregational singing in America."

Epilogue

One of Andrew Rozalowsky's last electronic updates quoted from the song "Praise the Lord" by The City Harmonic.[1] The song calls people to praise the Lord during every circumstance of life, from the heights of pleasure to the depths of pain. It proclaims that, "There is always grace enough today to Praise the Lord." On his deathbed, Andrew wanted everyone to know that, by God's grace, he was still, every day, able to praise the Lord. His spiritual and emotional peace, when combined with the rationality and coherence of the Christian worldview, provided an incredibly persuasive and compelling defence of his faith. Like countless others, Andrew's life and death demonstrated that Christianity is a worldview that is both intellectually acceptable and existentially livable.

Every believer—as well as the real Christian church corporately—is called to live out the truth of the gospel with head, heart and hands.

---

[1] The City Harmonic. "Praise the Lord" from the album, *Heart* (2013).

When transformed hearts and minds move the hands to produce the fruit of active, self-sacrificial love, the rational defence of the Christian faith is placed in a gloriously attractive and reinforcing framework. Christ demands our every faculty, and then releases us into the world to defend the truth of the gospel with all that we are and have. When we do so, we find that the gospel produces an intellectual, emotional, existential and spiritual resonance deep inside our being.

Andrew Rozalowsky lived out his life, sickness and death in a way which lovingly shouted the reality of the gospel through the quiet whisper of his character. The way he conducted himself plainly showed that his hope in Jesus was a transforming hope. Perhaps more accurately, it showed that his hope was in a transforming Saviour. Andrew didn't merely *say* he trusted in Jesus, he *demonstrated* it. He lived it. He died it. Because of his faith-union with the Lord Jesus Christ, he will live in it forevermore. His experience, though particular, shares the universal truth of the gospel.

Although God calls his children to live out their faith in unique situations, they all share the same Lord and Saviour. By the grace of God, may all of us who follow Christ learn to proclaim and defend our faith in both word and deed, in the situations where God places us and in all the circumstances of our lives. And, as Andrew wanted me to remember, may everything we think, feel, say and do, be stamped with *Soli Deo gloria—to God alone be the glory!*

Andrew Rozalowsky
(April 28, 1984–January 6, 2014)

Appendix:
A patient hope

This appendix consists of a sermon preached by Andrew Rozalowsky on November 25, 2012, which he entitled, "A groaning creation and a patient hope: My story with cancer." Andrew was well-prepared and spoke from organized notes, but he did not write out a full manuscript. For this appendix, the decision was made to reproduce his sermon the way he actually spoke it. Even though this type of oral communication results in grammatical irregularities that would be ironed out in writing, it was decided to retain as much of the feel of the sermon as possible. Only in a few places has the sermon been lightly edited. Many thanks are due to Jesskah Farquharson for diligently and accurately transcribing the sermon audio for this chapter:

WELL, YES, Pastor Steve, the friendship is mutual. And I think I have the advantage because I can pronounce your last name a little bit easier.

But, it's a wonderful privilege to be here with you this morning. I am a member at Calvary Baptist Church (that Steve just mentioned) here in Guelph along with my wife Suzanne, who's here, and we have a history with this church [Crestwicke Baptist Church] as well. Suzanne actually became a Christian in this very room—eight years ago now?

And, I think she was baptized there [*pointing*], if I recall correctly. She was coming here when she was in university and I believe it was in her second year. So, at that point, she had been coming a number of times before she was a Christian—and hearing the gospel in this very room and from this very church and through the preaching of the Word on the university campus, as well. And so it was this very room, on a February morning, that she came to know the Lord. So, I'm very grateful for this church and the faithfulness of the preaching of it over the years.

Now, Pastor Steve has given me two tasks this morning. The first one, of course, is the primary task and that is to preach the Word. And so that's what I'm going to do, but the second is to share my own life story as I do preach the Word.

And so I'll be preaching from Romans 8:18–25, and I'll be illustrating it by sharing with you my own personal journey. So it'll be a little bit of a different message for me, as I speak about myself a little more often than I might on other occasions. So turn with me to Romans 8:18. And I'll be reading here.

> I consider that our present sufferings are not worth comparing with the glory that will be revealed in us. The creation waits in eager expectation for the children of God to be revealed. For the creation was subjected to frustration, not by its own choice, but by the will of the one who subjected it, in hope that the creation itself will be liberated from its bondage to decay and brought into the freedom and glory of the children of God. We know that the whole creation has been groaning as in the pains of childbirth right up to the present time. Not only so, but we ourselves, who have the firstfruits of the Spirit groan inwardly as we wait eagerly for our adoption to sonship, the redemption of our bodies. For in this hope we were saved. But hope that is seen is no hope at all. Who hopes for what they already have? But if we hope for what we do not yet have, we wait for it patiently.

This is God's Word.

The apostle Paul, in this text, is a realist. He plainly talks about the world as he sees it and as, I think, you and I see it as well. He talks about *present sufferings*—verse 18, creation being *subjected to frustration*—verse 20, the need for liberation in the face of its bondage to decay—verse 21. He plainly states that we know that the whole creation has been groaning as in the pains of childbirth, right up to the present time—verse 22.

It won't take much to establish this notion in the present day with respect to creation. How do you approach it? Are you a realist, like Paul is? Earthquakes demolish cities and cripple nations. Haiti is one recent example, Japan another. And I think both of our churches—Calvary and Crestwicke—support missionaries that serve in Japan. I don't know if you follow the Saddlers [missionaries sent from Guelph to Japan] at all, but it's been *chilling* following the tales of the tremors that have continued to rock them and amazing, as well, to see the opportunities for the gospel to go out throughout the nation of Japan. But nonetheless, I think we can tell that through earthquakes and through other natural phenomena, the world isn't quite as we think it should be. So, on a global level, it doesn't take much to establish that.

Or, we're quite familiar with the groaning of creation on a human-to-human level. Already the Israel-Gaza conflict has been mentioned this morning, and I think this is a good example of no matter what you think of the political issues involved, deep down, there are sin issues, there's violence, there's a lack of peace. This is not a lack of groaning, this is groaning. This is a groaning creation on a human-to-human level.

But it's not as though this groaning of creation and this suffering only applies to creation on broad levels and it's something "out there" that we don't really have to think about too much. It's beyond us. And we as Christians, who have the Spirit, are somehow immune to it. Look back at verse 23. Paul applies this notion of a groaning creation to *us* who are children of God and who have the Spirit. Not only so, but we ourselves who have the firstfruits of the Spirit groan *inwardly* as we wait eagerly for our adoption, the redemption of our bodies.

Now, suffering and the groaning of creation, on a personal level as a Christian, takes many forms. My own experience resonates with Paul's words. It was a year ago this month—November—that I developed a blood clot in my left leg. So I went to a walk-in clinic in town, one Saturday morning, and told them what was the matter, and they said, "We think you need to go to the ER right away—sounds like a blood clot." So I went off to the Guelph ER [emergency room], had bloodwork done, had an ultrasound on the leg, and it was found that it was just a superficial clot and so there was no immediate danger posed to my life. I was put on anti-inflammatories and from there I would just carry on.

So I went home, carried on with life and slowly it kind of progressed and by mid-November, I'd gone back to the ER again, just to see if anything had gotten worse. And again they said that it was a superficial blood clot, it wasn't going to pose any problems/immediate danger to my life and sent me home. But he did mention one thing—the ER doctor, that is—he said, "Your white blood cell count was a little high last time. It might represent something of a blood disorder but follow up with your doctor."

OK. Um…that was a little scary to hear: "a blood disorder." So I went to my doctor, and it seemed to be easily explainable with the fact that white blood cell counts rise when you have inflammation in your body: it was trying to fight something. So I had a blood clot, white blood cells go up, fair enough. So, I kind of put it behind me.

Time carried on, though, and I moved into December. And finally, three days before Christmas 2011, I developed a blood clot in my other leg—my right leg. Now that's strange because you think once you develop something in another part of your body, in the exact same way, that there's got to be something underlying to actually cause that problem.

So, I went to my doctor, had some bloodwork done (it's, again, three days before Christmas) and then went home. Next morning, I'm working at home from a laptop and almost forgot anything, really, was going on. So now, we're Friday morning, two days before Christmas, and I get a phone call: a man is on the line asking for me and I don't recognize the voice, but he introduces himself as a GP [general practitioner] from my doctor's office (my GP was off that day). So he called and just said he needed to get in touch with me right away. He'd received my blood results and so he started to tell me what was going on. He started explaining what blast cells were and why they were in my blood stream. He began telling me about my red cells and my white cells and those sorts of numbers, and as he started to talk about these things, it slowly sunk in that something grave was the matter.

I sort of went into this state of what I could almost explain as paralysis, as I'm just barely hanging on to the words of this doctor and starting—everything in my body—just sort of shutting down and this adrenaline kind of taking over my head. And so my mind kind of came back into focus as I heard him say, "It looks like you have leukemic processes happening in your blood. I've arranged for you to meet with the hematologist this afternoon in Kitchener—but you have to go right now for blood work."

So that was the phone call. It came as somewhat of a shock because I'm sitting there thinking, "I'm a young man, seemingly healthy, and now I'm being told to drop everything, run to Kitchener for bloodwork and meet with a hematologist, a blood specialist, this afternoon at a cancer centre."

I managed to get off the phone, move upstairs where my wife and my son (who was one-and-a-half years old at the time) were, and just barely get upstairs, starting to sob and not really getting out any words whatsoever but trying to express: "I…I think…they think…I have… leukemia." So that there was a whirlwind day.

For some silly reason, I decided that I would run off to Kitchener first to get my bloodwork, while Suzanne had our son Jacob there at home and tried to figure out what to do with him for the day. I went back and forth between Guelph and Kitchener and met with the doctor a couple of times. By the end of the day, we had a suspected diagnosis; they had to send my blood work off to St. Michael's Hospital in Toronto, and that night we came back and she told me, "It looks like you have acute myeloid leukemia, which is a fast-moving, aggressive cancer of the blood." So you can imagine my wife and I sitting there, getting that news and what a shock it was, because, I don't know—young men don't usually go around expecting cancer to hit at any one time.

But, nonetheless, that was the situation we found ourselves in and this is two days before Christmas. And then I'm told, "Well, you'd better go home, grab your stuff; you're going to be sleeping here tonight." So I wouldn't be going home, to sleep in my own home and that itself was a little bit shocking as well, because you don't wake up in the morning thinking that you're not going to be sleeping in your own bed again for some time—and I didn't know how long it would be.

Really, I was told that (when I was trying to get a sense of the import of the gravity of this situation) some people, upon this diagnosis of acute myeloid leukemia, would have passed away within two days of that diagnosis. So I don't know if I have two days, three days, a week or a few weeks. It would have been at most, at that point, only a few weeks because it was taking over my body.

By the time I had a bone marrow biopsy—normally bone marrow is liquid and they can withdraw it; mine had to be chipped out because it was hardened—I was very close to death at this point. And being physically drained from all that, the state of the cancer taking over my body and the many needles (and I'm awful with needles so I sometimes find it kind of funny that I got a blood cancer of all things when I'm so squirmy with blood). But, nonetheless, I *did* get that sort of blood cancer. And then I had to go through chemotherapy which, as you probably know, are just very hard drugs.

But in the midst of all this, I still had time to think and the capacity to feel. So, young man, a wife, a son—and I don't know if I'm going to live out the week. And you know what was hard about that: thinking about not seeing my son get married, just as my dad didn't get to see me get married. He died nine years ago of brain cancer. It was hard thinking about my wife moving on without me there to support the family. These are tough thoughts, tough things to feel in the midst of being told that you might only have a few days to a few weeks to live. "We're going to try to treat you and do what we can but no promises. This…this is a blood cancer."

I suppose there are several ways to respond to this: emotionally, intellectually, and there's the *Why me?* approach. If you don't believe in God, it might take a certain form. If you do believe in God, it seems to take the form of *Why me, God? Why did you let this happen to me? I thought you were in control and good.* Or it might express, *Why do I deserve this?* Bound up with this might be the experience of anger (anger at God); or despair ("everything is hopeless"), or even doubt, something we don't like to probably talk about as Christians (experiencing doubt as to God's goodness, maybe the attributes and character of God in the midst of the suffering, or maybe his very existence—I don't know). And, these responses are understandable enough, when you're faced with seemingly your whole life crashing in upon you.

But recall the text we're in, in Romans. I've isolated, to this point, one aspect of it: the groaning creation. But just to stay on the groaning creation would be to fail to actually appreciate Paul's words in the text. It's not as though Paul says, "The world is cursed. Sickness is a fact. Death is real. Cancer kills. Oh, well—get over it or embrace it."

So, let's read the text again and see how Paul answers the problem of the groaning creation:

> I consider that our present sufferings are not worth comparing with the glory that will be revealed in us. For the creation waits in *eager* expectation for the *children of God* to be revealed. For the creation was subjected to frustration, not by its own choice, but by the will of the one who subjected it, *in hope* that the creation itself will be liberated from its bondage to decay and brought into the freedom and glory of the children of God. We know that the whole creation has been groaning as in the pains of childbirth right up to the present time. Not only so, but we ourselves, who have the firstfruits of the Spirit, groan inwardly as we wait *eagerly* for our adoption to sonship, the redemption of our bodies. For in this hope we were saved. But hope that is seen is no hope at all. Who hopes for what they already have? But if we hope for what we do not have, we wait for it patiently.

Doesn't sound to me like Paul is saying, "Oh well, death kills. It's a reality—get over it or embrace it." So what is this hope? *What is the hope?*

In the first place, Paul is saying that though the creation groans, though suffering exists in its many forms, there is coming a day where this will be reversed. There is *hope* for the redeeming of all creation. But note carefully: Paul isn't just saying that suffering and chaos will cease. He is saying that and surely that is a good thing—wouldn't we all love to see suffering, and the chaos that this world is in, gone, eradicated?

But if *all* we had was the lack of suffering, do we actually have anything positive? Anecdotally, as I look around in the world, I'm not sure that those that aren't in the appearance of suffering at the moment are necessarily the happiest people either, the most joyous people. I think that if all we had was a lack of suffering and a lack of chaos, we would not be fulfilling our purposes as human beings. And where, ultimately, would that leave us in relation to God? Would that do anything, if we were lacking in suffering? No. There's more in the text.

This hope that Paul talks about is bound up with the greater context of Paul's letter to the Romans. It's not just that we have hope that creation will one day be redeemed and suffering will cease. That's good, but it's not ultimate. This hope is bound up with something even more profound: the life, death, and resurrection of Jesus Christ.

On a big picture level, suffering exists because the creation has been cursed—and the creation has been cursed because of human rebellion against God. This is the story of Genesis 3. So, how does this problem, this sin problem, get solved? What you and I need is not moral preaching, moral teaching, telling you to do this and do that. There are biblical imperatives, certainly. But is that the way to solve the sin problem? If you read Romans 1–3, I don't think so. *None* is righteous! No, not one. What you and I need is *redemption*. What we need is *salvation*, not the lack of suffering. We need God to take care of our sin problem, and this he does through Jesus.

It is because Jesus died on the cross, taking on our sins, that we could be justified and forgiven. It is because Jesus rose from the dead that death has been conquered and we will one day be without suffering and be—even more importantly—in the presence of God forever. The New Jerusalem, the new heavens, and the new earth that are described for us in Revelation 21 and 22 are expressed to us in the symbolism of a cube. When the city is measured, it's said that it is as long as it is wide, and then—something strange—as high as it is long and wide. Now, if you picture that, that's—I think I calculated it before—that's a city that goes from the earth into space four to five times higher than the International Space Station orbits the earth. I can't picture walls like that.

But if you track the symbolism of the Book of Revelation, I think what John the writer is actually communicating to us is something more profound. The cube—what is the only cube found in the Old Testament? The only cube, it's the Holy of Holies in the tabernacle. The Holy of Holies in the temple. And do you recall what the Holy of Holies represented? It was *God's* dwelling place on earth. It was where *God* met with His people. John, in Revelation, is telling us that one day we will be *forever, ultimately, fully* in the presence of *God*. That is a *lovely, amazing, wonderful thing* to look forward to. It says earlier in the text, in Revelation 21, there will be no more tears, no more suffering, essentially. That is wonderful, but even more wonderful is where John goes with that to say that we will be the presence of God. That is what we were ultimately created for, to live and to find our purpose in him.

Though there was an element of shock in my diagnosis (like I said, young men don't go around just waiting for doctors to call saying they have cancer), I still had this underlying *peace* that day, a *patient hope*. I had to trust God with my life in that moment and know that *he is good, no matter what happens*. I had the very real possibility that I was not going to live out the week, or the month. Maybe some of you have been there yourselves, or with family members. I know there's been tragedy in this church as well and as I share my own story, I recognize that this is one story among many.

And it's strange, thinking back now, a year later, trying to recall what I was actually thinking upon getting my diagnosis. I worry sometimes that I might skew how I was really doing. I used Facebook as a way of communicating with friends while I was in the hospital. And, on Christmas Day, I wrote this message, and I share this simply to help you see the God that is behind this, not my strength or anything like that (and I'll come back to that in a moment). But this is what I wrote on Christmas Day to my friends (after we'd shared the news already in person with family members):

> *If you've noticed the messages here for me, you might have thought something was up. The news is: I was diagnosed with leukemia on Friday. It's aggressive so I start chemo on Tuesday. It's safe to say I was prepared for this. How? The first true thing to say is that God prepared me for it. The second is that my theology prepared me for this. (Aside: I'll explain that soon but I go on…) Suffering in this life is a reality, brought about in a world in rebellion against God. But thankfully it will one day be over and for now Jesus is my strength and my light. So instead of asking, "Why me?" I thought, Why not me? I hope to show how Jesus is sufficient for all things, through this. He truly is.*

By God's grace, I was ready for this. I knew the reality of sickness and death, the groaning creation. So I had no illusions about the longevity of my life. I had come up against this enough. As I mentioned, my dad had died—from this point it's nine years ago—from brain cancer. All my grandparents died young. I've seen some close to me die of cancer and other things.

But, you know what? Physical death no longer rears its ugly face of condemnation because Christ has redeemed us. There must be hope. There is hope of redemption and not just hope of redemption globally. It's not just that the Israel-Gaza conflict will one day be over, it's not just that the wars throughout the world will one day be over, but that you and I have been *redeemed by God* to be in relationship with him again, to be whole people loving God and being loved by God. That's what we're most in need of: this redemption and salvation, to have this hope. And, as Paul calls it, it's a *patient* hope because as we know, sickness still happens. Suffering still occurs. We were told this morning—we were praying for the Hannas and their news of cancer just recently. Others, probably, in this congregation with similar things—it doesn't have to be cancer—could be all sorts of things that we struggle with and we suffer through.

But Paul calls it a *patient hope* because the fullness of our salvation has not yet come. But it one day will come. There is a future glorification that Paul talks about in this text, if you go on and read the rest of Romans chapter 8, a *beautiful* chapter. There is a future hope for *all* of this to be brought together, and we will be, as I mentioned earlier, in the full presence of God, in the Holy of Holies with God forever.

I want to quickly highlight four things that I've either learned or had cemented as a result of this last year and in light of our text in Romans this morning. And then I'll bring things to a close.

> (1) We prepare to suffer before we've ever suffered. We don't do this through dwelling on suffering, necessarily, but through the establishing of the way that we think about God and that we understand God and that we experience God, we get ready to respond to God when you do get that call. Will you scramble to find hope when you are faced with your own mortality? Or will you already know where to go? Will you know that the right move is to turn to Jesus?
>
> (2) I've been blessed to see this suffering as a gift. James in his letter in the New Testament writes to consider our *trials* as *pure joy*—strange language, isn't it, considering trials to be pure joy? But I've experienced this last year that suffering can be a gift. My marriage has been strengthened; my love for my wife has been strengthened through this time, my love for family, my son; the experience of the prayers of God's people, the impact that that has had on my faith and my life has been astounding—and I make no illusions thinking that I got through this cancer to where I am now because of something I've done or something I've believed.

(3) Suffering presents an opportunity to make much of Jesus to a world that is in need of hope. When all is stripped away and you're facing death square in the face, what or who will you cling to? What or who offers what you most need? I've been blessed to get to share the gospel through this experience over the last year in ways I never expected to. That's made it more than worth going through.

(4) This is *my* journey. It may not look like yours. Not only are there several different types of suffering, there are different ways that we handle it. And I don't want to give the impression that the way that I've been able—by God's grace—to go through this is the only way, and you should feel guilty if you've had any other thoughts throughout that process. We are frail human beings in need of God's grace at all times, always needing to look to him for strength so that if we've expressed doubt, if we express despair, if we've expressed anger…we still turn to God. We still say to God, "We need you and we need your wonderful grace."

So what I want you to see about my story is that it is not me but the God who is behind it. I want you to see the sufficiency of Christ in all things, for all things. It was not *my* hope that sustained me. It was my hope in *God* and what Jesus had done on the cross and through his resurrection. It's what *objectively happened* almost two thousand years ago.

I purposely said nothing to this point about where my story went physically after January though I know that you are smart people and you've probably guessed that my presence here this morning, in speaking to you, means that, well, I'm alive and I must be doing well. The reason for waiting to do that, apart from what you could already gather, was that I wanted you to hear this message the same way that you would have heard it if I weren't alive to tell it, if someone else were telling it on my behalf. Or the way it was being experienced in the midst of the initial diagnosis and being in the hospital throughout December and January last year. Being in a hospital bed, having drugs pumped into me. I want you to know that there is, in all circumstances of life, and in all types of suffering, a hope—a patient hope—for the redemption of our bodies, for the redeeming of all creation, and especially for the redeeming of the relationship with God that was lost at the Fall and that we read about in Genesis 3.

So, just to complete the story, the first round of chemo did put me into remission. Which means, at that point, at the end of January, I had less than five percent leukemic cells in my blood and my bone marrow. I went through three more rounds of chemo that took me into April and then the recovering from that process into May, and then the recovery process has really taken me up until recently.

I've been blessed to return to school this semester [at McMaster Divinity School] and take one course and be able to research and write. I'm in biblical studies so it's been a blessing to me to be able to try to contribute to the church that way. And I praise God that I'm alive today.

But I still have a fifty per cent chance of relapse. It could happen. My bloodwork Friday came back perfectly normal—praise God for that. But you know what? Could be a year, could be five years; Lord willing, it could be twenty or thirty. I don't know. And you know what? That's not going to bother me. I have a hope in a good and gracious, *sovereign* God in control over all things. I have a patient hope knowing that the redemption of our bodies and the redemption of the relationship will come. And, that's a message worth sharing with a dying and hurting world around us. There is hope. And it's found in our Lord and Saviour Jesus Christ. Let's pray.

> Father, this has been one amazing experience, this last little bit, preparing for this message and re-experiencing some of the emotions that I've had throughout the last year and that my wife and I dealt with last December. I thank You, Father, for how You have been a present hope, a present peace. You have provided Your love and You continue to provide Your love in this congregation; amidst all sorts of suffering, You are there. And Lord, if there are those here this morning that do not know You and know that peace, I pray, Father, You would work and show by Your Spirit the magnificence of Your glory. Show the sufficiency of Christ in all things, that though we are beaten, though this creation groans, Christ is sufficient. Christ is all we need. And we look forward, Lord, to the day when you bring this all to completion and Your glory be made known throughout all the earth, and every knee would bow and confess that You are Lord and God, King over all the earth. In Jesus' name. Amen.